The Naval Institute Almanac of the U.S. Navy

Titles in the Blue & Gold Series

The Bluejacket's Manual
The Chief Petty Officer's Guide
Reef Points
Career Compass
Watch Officer's Guide
Division Officer's Guide
Ethics for the Junior Officer
The Naval Officer's Guide
Command at Sea
American Admiralship
Naval Ceremonies, Customs, and Traditions
Dictionary of Naval Abbreviations
Dictionary of Naval Terms
Dictionary of Modern Strategy and Tactics
The Naval Institute Guide to Naval Writing
A Sailor's History of the U.S. Navy
Naval Shiphandler's Guide
Dutton's Nautical Navigation
Farwell's Rules of the Nautical Road

Forthcoming Titles

Petty Officer's Manual
Newly Commissioned Officer's Guide
Dutton's Navigation Dictionary
Submarine Officer's Guide
Mariner's Guide to Meteorology
Mariner's Guide to Oceanography

Naval Institute Press
291 Wood Road
Annapolis, MD 21402

Library of Congress Cataloging-in-Publication Data
Cowden, Anthony, 1962–
The Naval Institute almanac of the U.S. Navy / Anthony Cowden.
    p. cm. (The U.S. Naval Institute blue & gold professional
library)
Includes index.
ISBN 1-59114-131-1 (alk. paper)
1. United States. Navy—Handbooks, manuals, etc. 2. United
States. Navy—History—21st century. 3. Iraq War, 2003– —
Naval operations, American. 4. Iraq War, 2003– —Aerial opera-
tions, American.
I. United States Naval Institute. II. Title. III. Series.
  VA58.4.C7 2006
  359'.00973--dc22

                                            2005020846

Printed in the United States of America on acid-free paper ∞

12 11 10 09 08 07 06 05   9 8 7 6 5 4 3 2
First printing

The Naval Institute Almanac of the U.S. Navy

Anthony Cowden

Naval Institute Press
Annapolis, Maryland

The U.S. Naval Institute Blue & Gold Professional Library

For more than a hundred years, U.S. Navy professionals have counted on specialized books published by the Naval Institute Press to prepare them for their responsibilities as they advance in their careers and to serve as ready references and refreshers when needed. From the days of coal-fired battleships to the era of unmanned aerial vehicles and laser weaponry, such perennials as *The Bluejacket's Manual* and the *Watch Officer's Guide* have guided generations of Sailors through the complex challenges of naval service. As these books are updated and new ones are added to the list, they will carry the distinctive mark of the Blue & Gold Professional Library series to remind and reassure their users that they have been prepared by naval professionals and they meet the exacting standards that Sailors have long expected from the U.S. Naval Institute.

BLUE & GOLD
PROFESSIONAL LIBRARY

To Lt. Cdr. Henry E. Mooberry,
U.S. Naval Sea Cadet Corps,
for the leadership example
and opportunities he has provided
for the youth of Washington, D.C.,
over these many years.

Contents

Part Three. Touchstones

Foreword

Almanacs are defined as "lists, charts, and tables of useful information in many unrelated fields." This almanac is different. Its contents are all related to why we have a Navy: to project credible combat power to the far corners of the earth; to ensure U.S. sovereignty; and to provide options for the president . . . anywhere, anytime, without a permission slip!

This is an almanac of our Navy at war.

The War on Terrorism is well into its third year, and Operation Iraqi Freedom is moving into its second year. These operations have left an indelible mark on our military and future vision for joint war fighting. During this time we, as a nation, have achieved a number of successes, but much work in the War on Terrorism, and in securing Iraq's long-term prosperity and liberty, remains before us.

In early 2001, the idea that America would be engaged in two major combat operations in the span of the next two years seemed very unlikely. In particular, the concept of an America engaged in a long-term global war against terror was a notion of novelists and academic theorists. The events of September 11, however, shook our worldview and forced a major reformulation of our perceptions. Perhaps the most important lesson for the military and our nation's leaders was the reminder that the only constant in today's world is uncertainty, and that America must be postured to protect not only its interests overseas, but also to defend the homeland.

The U.S. Navy and the Marine Corps team have a proud and distinguished history of responding to our nation's call during uncertain and challenging times. Our expeditionary heritage is inherently woven into our day-to-day operations, and as you will see in this almanac, there are a number of modern, compelling accounts of how we continue to demonstrate our flexibility and agility in defense of our national security. Additionally, within this almanac you will find moving descriptions of how heroic decisions and action by our personnel are, and will remain, a hallmark of the Navy story, be that in hostile waters abroad or in defense of hearth and home.

Our recent combat operation successes reinforce the value of maritime power and the need for credible and capable naval forces. This nation's wise and sustained investment in Navy capabilities enabled us to be ready when the president ordered our forces into harm's way. At the same time, the Department of the Navy's commitment to an expanding range of capabilities, from maritime dominance to precision strike, from littoral warfare to power projection, will ensure our ability to meet future challenges.

To maintain our capacity to respond and provide sovereign and purposeful presence in forward regions across the globe, we must continuously evaluate our processes of training, equipping, and organizing ourselves to engage the certain threats of today, and more importantly, the uncertain threats of tomorrow. In our survey we must learn the right lessons from our distant and recent past. In this sense, our examination of Operations Enduring Freedom and Iraqi Freedom is a commitment to accurately recording our recent history of operations in the war on terror in order to guide our forces' performance for the future. We are charting our course with imagination, tempered by experience.

It is a maritime maxim that in order to know where you are headed, you must know your current location, direction, and speed of movement—that is, get a "fix" on where you are. Accordingly, this almanac will be a baseline fix that provides a detailed assessment of our forces and our Navy organization today. We in the maritime services must incorporate such tools into our evaluations and assessments if we are to plan properly to respond to threats of today and tomorrow.

For Navy personnel, this almanac will serve as an important reference as you consider how your experiences fit into the larger context of national security. For observers of the Navy, it can serve as a touchstone for better understanding the dynamic maritime operational environment and for gaining a detailed appreciation of the diverse components and capabilities of the finest maritime force in the world's history.

Our Sailors are rightly proud of their accomplishments and should be praised for their service and sacrifice. We must not be content with the successes we have achieved, however. Rather, we must keep our eyes on the horizon, remaining vigilant for the inevitable storms and poised to navigate uncertain seas.

> Vice Adm. Kevin P. Green
> Deputy Chief of Naval Operations
> for Plans, Policy, and Operations
> (OPNAV N3/N5)

Acknowledgments

The author is indebted to a wide range of individuals who helped make this book possible. At the risk of leaving someone out, the author would like to thank Tom Cutler of the U.S. Naval Institute, who urged me to pursue this project; the contributing authors who have provided articles and sections of the book—Vice Adm. Kevin P. Green, Capt. Edward "Sonny" Masso, Lt. Garrett D. Kasper, Vice Adm. David L. Brewer III, Cdr. William P. Bradley, YN2 Sam D. Sluka III, Rear Adm. (lower half) William Crowder, and Rear Adm. (lower half) Bruce B. Engelhardt; Capt. Neil Hogg; Cdr. Robert Girrier; the staff at the Naval Institute, especially Jennifer Till Wallace, who was instrumental in assembling the ship and aircraft photos; Michael Bailey of Sonalysts, Inc.; and my lovely bride, Suzanne, who put up with my early risings and late hours during the writing of this book.

The author would also like to thank all those who have purchased this book, and he invites them to send any comments to him at navalalmanac@snet.net.

The Naval Institute Almanac
of the U.S. Navy

Part One

Focus On

A Look Back   1

9/11 from the View of Naval Reserve Navy Command Center Detachment 106

Capt. Edward "Sonny" Masso, USNR, a select reservist, is a 1977 graduate of the University of Mississippi and its NROTC program. He presently serves as deputy commander, Naval Surface Force, U.S. Atlantic Fleet, and is employed by the Anteon Corporation.

It had been a busy two years in Naval Reserve (NR) Navy Command Center (NCC) Detachment 106. The frenetic pace since October 1999 had included numerous "no-notice" crisis action team (CAT) responses as well as significant personnel turnover in the OPNAV N3/5 organization that kept my unit in a perpetual state of change—and in a perpetual quest to be trained and ready for any possible call for service.

The Legacy NCC 106 Unit

The unit was more than a hundred strong, mostly officers. My crew had representatives from fourteen states, as far away as California. Our nineteen captains served as Navy Department duty captains (NDDCs) and were ably assisted by more than twenty-five commanders and another twenty-five lieutenant commanders. Twelve to fifteen lieutenants rounded out the wardroom.

At the beginning of my tenure, duties of the unit included CAT support, duty captain, and assistant duty officer watch standing in the command center—in close proximity to the offices of the chief of naval operations (CNO) and the secretary of the navy (SECNAV), as well as CNO/senior officer briefers, political-military specialists, and other action-officer support professionals. The thirty-plus enlisted personnel included graphic support personnel, information technology specialists, and other watch-standing support rates such as operations specialist, yeoman, personnel specialists, and an odd array of other rates served by only the finest personnel available.

NCC 106 manned nearly 30 percent of the command center watches, augmenting the post-major command captains who rotated through the other 70 percent of watch-standing duties. The pace alternated between periods of boredom, to fast-paced and exciting "tip of the spear"–type support. In no particular order, we were called to stand up CATs for the Egypt Air disaster in New England, the USS *Cole,* the USS *Greeneville* collision, the EP-3 collision over China, and several very politically sensitive incidents at the Vieques training range, as well as providing action officer, planning, and/or watch-stander support for Y2K contingencies, the Quadrennial Defense Review, and Exercise Top Official (TOPOFF).

Early in my tenure, we were organized like most major staffs with N1 (administration), N2 (intelligence), N3 (current operations), N4 (logistics), N5 (planning), and so on, assistant chiefs of staff. A typical drill weekend would find nearly 80 percent of the unit involved in current operations briefs, staff support work (to the OPNAV staff), unit administration support, and other training-related endeavors.

The mantra of the command vision and climate was pretty basic, learned from my first department head, then-Lt. Bill Keating Jr., to train (hard) for the unknown and to be able to execute our duties in the exact manner in which we trained if the need should arise. Repetition breeds confidence. Under duress this confidence would be needed to ensure proper execution. Another Bill Keating lesson followed from my observation of his command of USS *Fife* (DD-991) and USS *Chancellorsville* (CG-62)—make your Assistant Chiefs of Staff (ACOSs) (department heads) the "captains" of their departments, or staffs. Instill ownership, delegate, and expect the best.

This direction to the highly motivated men and women of NCC 106 yielded effective results. The ACOSs focused on several issues: (a) the potential of an asymmetrical threat disabling the command center and what we would do in response; (b) the creation of highly innovative exercises that would test our ability to execute whatever functions we were expected to perform; and (c) training the entire command to perform multiple functions (this training was command wide and intense). Goals and objectives for our training were carefully monitored, with careful consideration of how multiple ACOSs integrated with each other while performing diverse tasks.

A brief example was a study of the potential for possible evacuation to Site R, the alternate command center. If, hypothetically, a foreign chemical agent were present in close proximity to the NCC, which resulted in a need to transfer control to Site R, would we know how to respond? Did our personnel know how to find Site R, located in a remote location a significant distance away from the Pentagon? Would our security clearances and badges be on file at Site R when we arrived? Did we know our way around the site in a comfortable manner so that we would immediately be able to find our work location and perform our duties? Was the information technology (IT) environment similar to the actual command center? Were the databases similar and seamless?

All these premises were tested and the results reported to the front office. We developed a very close personal working relationship with the government service professionals who operate Site R. We integrated our efforts with the three other OPNAV N3/5 augmentation units (including the Site R unit). We chose several "Fast Team" members to drive to Site R from the Pentagon (on a stop watch), their homes, and their places of employment so that directions were not necessary to locate this remote command facility. We also established and tested numerous ways to communicate with one another, with complex call plans and ACOSs accountable for knowing where their personnel were at nearly all times.

A Unit Faces and Embraces Change

Within six months of my tenure Rear Adm. John Byrd and his Executive Assistant (EA), Capt. Bud Jewett, posed a unique challenge to NCC 106. Could we stand more watches? Could we stand all the watches? How soon? What would be the consequences? The line of questions went to their desire to free up the post-major command captains for other OPNAV duties while relying on NCC 106 for additional support. Their entering arguments were simple: Priority one: watch standing and CAT support. Priority two: Site R augmentation. Priority three: everything else we had been doing.

Could NCC 106 become a 24/7/365-type command? Which current duties would we need to divest in order to support their stated priorities? Could a commander or lieutenant commander qualify for and handle the NDDC responsibilities? Change can be hard, but within months after concept agreement with the front office, NCC 106 was operating 24/7/365. We were enabled by the strong support of Capt. Keith Amacker's fine staff at the Navy Marine Corps Reserve Center, Washington, D.C.

The fifteenth of August 2001 found us in the brand-new command center in the newly renovated section of the Pentagon. We had participated in every level of planning for this critical move. That month, NCC 106 stood more than one hundred watches, doubling up for nearly an entire week in both the old and new command centers to ensure connectivity. The unit was divested of many political-military–type support functions and was now executing Admiral Byrd's vision under the leadership of Vice Adm. Tim Keating.

9/11/2001

I was at my desk in Crystal City around 0615 that day. I had a lot to do, both in my civilian job and in preparing for my end-of-the-month change of command. Lunch was planned in the SECNAV's mess, with a high school classmate, Col. John Kruse, USMC, serving as Secretary England's EA. I had to pick up my change of command invitations from Capt. Gerry DeConto in the command center. My plan was to stop by his desk around 1100 prior to meeting Colonel Kruse and Comdr. Brian Peter, USCG, for lunch.

At approximately 0830 the radio interrupted its normal programming and announced that a plane had struck the north tower of the World Trade Center in New York City. The details were sketchy, but in the course of half-listening, I originally believed a small plane hit the Trade Center tower due to pilot error. A few minutes later the radio clarified that the plane was a commercial jetliner that we would later learn was a Boeing 767, American Airlines Flight 11, originating from Boston.

I quickly placed a call to Capt. Larry Getzfred and to the Navy Department duty officer (NDDO), Lt. Comdr. Ron Vauk, to see what they knew and if they required assistance. The feedback was that they were still in the data-collection mode but to stand by. I then called my N3, Comdr. Gregg Marvil, to alert him of possible pending action. As I hung up from this call, I learned that at 0905 the south tower of the World Trade Center was struck by another Boeing 767, United Airlines Flight 175. I immediately departed for the mall entrance parking lot of the Pentagon to report to the command center.

My parking pass says that I passed through security at the mall entrance at 0930. I walked into the Pentagon and checked into the SECNAV's office to tell Colonel Kruse lunch might be in jeopardy. We watched the president on television for a minute or two, and I proceeded to the command center to assess what type of support the unit could offer. At the top of the escalator on the fourth floor, just above the A-Ring first-floor command center, I felt a sharp jolt and heard a loud noise that resembled a bomb or an earthquake. I raced down the escalator—the power was out—and found the scene eerie. It was dark, the overheads and bulkheads (ceilings and walls) had buckled, and there was a lot of smoke.

The world would later learn that at 0939 a Boeing 757, American Airlines Flight 77 from Dulles Airport, was the cause of this damage.

The only access I found to the command center was the open area between the A and B Rings, the backside of what was once the command center. There was a gaping hole in the wall from which flames and smoke poured. I could see the flames tickling the glass through the windows on the second and third floors, and personnel were pressing the glass in an attempt to escape. It was clear the windows were the only way out for these Army and civilian personnel.

The next thirty minutes or so were chaotic. My cell phone did not work. My RIM pager did work. I was able to send a generic email to my ACOSs—almost an "any station this net"–type of message alerting them to engage their personnel. Comdr. Val Eichenlaub would be my first contact from my RIM pager. She was on it. So was my N3, Commander Marvil, who resided in Miami, Florida. He had been on the phone with the command center when the line went dead. He had already contacted his deputy ACOS with instructions. Within minutes of learning that the Pentagon had been struck, several members of my unit had automatically deployed themselves to Site R. Captain Engvall; Commanders Bundo, Densford, Ryan, and Wetzel; and Lieutenant Commanders Maxwell, Cantwell, and McDonald were at Site R between ninety minutes and two-and-one-half hours after the act of war had occurred.

At the site of the disaster, it was uncharacteristically quiet. Personnel jumping from the higher floors were being caught by teams of volunteers who formed human safety nets. There were small teams of three or four personnel under several windows. Admiral Balisle and his team of heroes from OPNAV N76 arrived and began firefighting and more aggressive rescuing efforts. We were successful in extracting several individuals from the burning hole, but the heat and fire from the twenty-two thousand pounds of aviation fuel were too much for the meager but gallant efforts of the rescuers armed only with their courage and two minutes of fire-extinguisher power per unit. Several people on scene who had recently jumped from the second and third floors were in a state of panic. There were loud admonishments about a second aircraft threat inbound. The on-scene personnel did not waiver; they would leave only when relieved by professional rescuers.

In the meantime, the N3/5 team at OPNAV found a place to operate the command center. The NCC officially was shifted to and operated out of the Marine Corps Operations Command Center in the Navy Annex. Brig. Gen. Gordon Nash, USMC, was the consummate host. Several of my NDDOs had already reported to the annex to begin work.

To facilitate my unit command and control, I departed the scene around 1100. I could not exit the building to find my car for nearly thirty minutes due to the damage and secured accesses of passageways one would normally use to traverse the short distance to the mall entrance. After loaning my sporadically available cell phone to several senior officials of the Office of the Secretary of Defense, I departed for my office in Crystal City to further engage with my unit, N3/5, and assess our personnel casualties. I also started a recall within the office of the Assistant Secretary of the Navy for Research, Development, and Acquisition (ASN/RDA) chief engineer whose staff spends a lot of time between Crystal City and the Pentagon.

I received numerous calls en route to Crystal City from my ACOSs, each reporting status and actions taken. The normally five-minute drive was lengthened by the evacuation of the entire city in fear of additional attacks. My ACOSs were truly on the same wavelength with my every concern: (1) deployment to Site R; (2) deployment to the new command center in the Navy Annex; (3) whereabouts of all our personnel; (4) assessment of who was likely in the command center during the attack; (5) notification of personnel to further augment a CAT, National Military Command Center (NMCC), NDDO, or other support; and (6) notification of personnel to possibly serve as family support to any of our as of then unidentified missing or injured personnel.

My office was practically empty. I was using my second cell phone battery and was in constant contact with key persons from my unit and from OPNAV.

My Chief Staff Officer (CSO) was in England, as was my N8 (Anti-Terrorism/Force Protection ACOS)—each on a separate trip with their civilian employers. Comdr. Barb Sweredoski from my N1 shop became my CSO. Lt. Comdr. Bill Scaring would now be my N8. No gap went unfilled.

With a good sense that we were operationally engaged with OPNAV in all of their short-term requirements, it was now time to deal with the unthinkable—the casualties. In this matter there was no line between active, reserve, contractor support, or civil servant. We needed to adjudicate the missing personnel list. This was fairly easy for the reserves, as we exercise recall bills and procedures numerous times a year. This is rarely done for active forces; with the loudspeakers of the Pentagon exhorting evacuation, many people followed orders and left the area and were not in ready range for communications due to the lengthy drives home exacerbated by the heavier-than-normal traffic that day. Our challenge was to determine who else might be missing in addition to those personnel we knew were on watch.

I was one of several who made calls to the homes of those we weren't sure were in the command center. This was a difficult but important job. Within a few hours, we were largely confident of the list of personnel who were unaccounted for. For my NCC 106 personnel, I was uncomfortable relying on the Casualty Assistance and Calls Officer (CACO) process and designated several officers for this important family-support function. I was painfully aware that in every matter pertaining to this attack, my unit was completely trained to respond appropriately—with this as the only exception. We had never trained to deal with the families of unaccounted for and likely injured personnel. My guidance to these support officers was to treat these families exactly as they would want their families treated if the roles were reversed. These personnel performed brilliantly. Their key actions of support included: (1) be present in uniform at the homes of the missing; (2) prepare to stay at the home, even to sleep in the driveway, until they were relieved; (3) assist with CACO-type duties and be with the families during CACO visits; (4) call hourly to the quickly established 800-number at the Bureau of Naval Personnel (BUPERS) in Millington, Tennessee, to report status, changes, or other official information; (5) act as my liaison in any matter required by the family; and (6) provide assistance to next of kin in any way necessary.

The Next Day(s)

Site R was stood down as the CNO and N3/5 determined the threat to be sufficient to operate the command center from the Navy Annex. NCC 106 was supporting N3/5 in the following manner:

The NMCC Liaison—augmentation by four officers: Commanders Bundo, Wetzel, Adams, and Cowden

Battle Watch Captain (BWC) and CAT Watch Officers—several officers filling in for personnel losses from the attack

Augmentation in additional areas, such as medal writing, assisting in potential personnel recalls for any response, and assisting with general "crew rest"–type support for personnel who hadn't slept in several days.

Important liaison work on lessons learned from the strengths and weaknesses of Site R as an alternate command center, identifying what had worked and what needed to be improved.

Vice Adm. John Totushek, Commander of the Naval Reserve Force, personally contacted me and was visible to most of my unit throughout this arduous process. His deputy, Capt. Craig McDonald, rejected none of our requests; he was our conduit to providing all service and support requested by Admiral Keating and his leadership team at N3/5. All supporting personnel were placed on orders immediately. Captain McDonald extended every courtesy and support to families of our unaccounted for (and later-to-be-determined deceased) personnel. Active Duty for Special Word (ADSW) orders were written for the NMCC support team. Captain McDonald and his staff assisted us in finding the right reservists for specific special requests—one of which was to help create an interim command center as well as to support the efforts to construct a new operations center for the Navy. I spoke with Admiral Totushek nearly every day for the next two weeks. He

provided NCC 106 with 250 additional days of active duty training (ADT) from 9/11 to the end of the fiscal year.

As the days went on, we would learn that so many of our shipmates, colleagues, friends, and close associates had perished in the
attack: Gerry DeConto—a friend for nearly twenty years; Jack
Punches—the rock and foundation of our command center leadership for nearly five years as the EA to Admirals Parker, Carmichael,
and Utley; Lt. Eric Cranford; Commander Murphy; Capt. Larry
Getzfred; and two members of NCC 106—the NDDO during the
attack, Lieutenant Commander Vauk, and Lt. Comdr. Bob Elseth.
I could go on. None of our OPNAV N3/5 fallen shipmates will
ever be forgotten.   .

Ops Normal

As with any tragedy, a normal battle rhythm kicks in and no matter
how things have changed, no matter how sad or tired you are, daily
operations become routine. With routine comes humor. With humor
comes the release of pent-up tension, and with that comes the
restoration of the spirit that is the American military professional.
As we said good-bye to another shipmate almost daily, with full
military honors and appropriate personal decorations at Arlington
Cemetery, we found ourselves operating in a solid routine. CNO,
Vice CNO, and the N3/5 staff would soon move back to the Pentagon. Admiral Keating would shortly assume duties as Commander
5th Fleet. Rear Adm. James M. Zortman would soon transfer to his
Strike Battle Group. Capt. Jeff Lemmons would soon relieve me
and would ably carry the ball to the next level of support.

Looking back, I am awed by the talent and professionalism of
NCC 106. Throughout every crisis the bar was raised for every reservist to emulate. Relevancy, flexibility, adaptability, and battle-
mindedness have become watchwords for all reservists in the key
support units. There are amazing stories of other great reserve support from the units supporting Fifth Fleet and Central Command
(CENTCOM), from Sixth Fleet in Gaeta, Italy, and from Seventh
Fleet in Yokosuka, Japan. The flyaway Joint Forces Air Component Command (JFACC) augment units had personnel in the air
toward the Middle East/Southwest Asia theater within days after
9/11.

On 4 October, I found myself in Ras El Tin, Egypt, serving as
chief of staff to Commander Task Force 150 in exercise Bright

Star. Several of my command center officers were with me, fresh from their service in the Pentagon. Bright Star was critical to demonstrating to moderate Arabs and the world that the United States had its chin up and could perform all duties and missions assigned. From 9/11 we segued into Bright Star, Operation Enduring Freedom, and hundreds of maritime interdiction operations (MIOs) in the theater. The total force concept—active and reservist working side by side—was in full effect. The long arm of democracy and justice, and the greatest military in the history of the world, demonstrated emphatically that Americans will endure any burden in defense of their country.

Ironies

The captain of American Airlines Flight 77, which hit the Pentagon, was a 1971 U.S. Naval Academy graduate and Navy captain named Chip Burlingame. He had retired from the naval service (from the NCC 106 unit) and was well known by many unit members. Rear Adm. Wilson "Bud" Flagg was a retired rear admiral who was a mentor to many of my officers and a dear friend to our reserve community. There were other victims from the four airline disasters who were well known to many of us and had strong ties to the Navy, and to NCC 106.

Two-plus years later the memories still linger. A segment of the American public has demonstrated that their memories of this attack on our soil have dulled. To those of us who were there that day, the memories have not faded. The experts are wrong. Time does not heal all wounds. We will never forget.

Around the World, Around the Clock   2

Operations Noble Eagle and Enduring Freedom

As it has for 226 years, your Navy has been fully engaged around the world, operating jointly with our fellow armed services and in concert with coalition partners including Operations Noble Eagle, Enduring Freedom, Iraqi Freedom, and the Global War on Terrorism. The U.S. Navy's enduring strength remains our men and women in uniform, who are provided for by the investment of the American people. Today, Sailors and Marines honor the faith of their countrymen as they stand watch over our nation and its allies around the world.

The Navy is organized by global areas of responsibility (AORs). The numbered fleets are responsible for specific areas. In each fleet there are ships involved in all kinds of activities: operations in support of the national strategy, building coalitions with our critical partners around the world who are en route to or from their deployments or conducting combat training. This also includes ships that are forward stationed in those areas. The Fifth Fleet covers Central Command's AOR. Ships in that area on any day might be involved in enforcing United Nations sanctions in the Arabian Gulf or maritime interdiction operations. The Sixth Fleet operates within European Command's AOR. In this area ships are conducting operations like the United Nations' peacekeeping missions in the Balkans and building coalitions with our regional partners. The Seventh Fleet operates within the Pacific Command's AOR, conducting joint operations with our Asian allies and conducting freedom of navigation operations. In the Sec-

This article is a condensed and edited version of the script for a multimedia CD-ROM developed for the Office of the Secretary of the Navy by Sonalysts, Inc.

ond Fleet, there are forces conducting drug interdiction operations and pre-deployment training, as well as manning the major U.S. naval bases. Third Fleet covers the other half of Pacific Command's AOR and completes our quick tour of the Navy world. Bottom line . . . the Navy provides credible combat power worldwide, 24/7/365.

On the morning of September 11, 2001, the Navy was in position around the world. The *Kitty Hawk* battle group and the *Essex* Amphibious Ready Group, or ARG as it is known, were forward stationed in Japan. The *Peleliu* ARG was engaged in exercises with the Royal Australian Navy. The *Enterprise* battle group was outbound from its deployment to the Arabian Gulf, and *Vinson* was inbound to relieve it. The *Kearsarge* ARG was conducting NATO exercises in the Mediterranean. The battle groups and ARGs from Second and Third Fleets were undergoing pre-deployment training and local operations.

September 11 began much like the tenth in terms of where the ships were located. But September 11 was anything but a "typical" day for the Navy—or for our nation.

Ships at sea around the world were ordered to their highest state of readiness.

On the home front, the ships that were under way or could immediately get to sea sortied to positions off the East and West Coasts. Carrier aircraft and surface combatants extended the arcs of air coverage normally provided by the North American Air Defense Command (NORAD) for hundreds of miles out to sea and established maritime defensives as well.

The hospital ship *Comfort* was sortied from Baltimore and sailed to New York where she was able to provide medical services as well as berthing for the relief workers from the southern tip of Manhattan.

In the North Arabian Sea, *Enterprise,* outbound from her deployment to the Arabian Gulf, immediately reversed course and headed back to the North Arabian Sea. *Vinson* made best speed to the North Arabian Sea. The six to ten ships in the typical carrier battle group include surface combatant and submarines, with additional strike and surveillance capabilities as well as support ships.

Over the next few weeks, the Navy, as part of a total joint force, prepared to conduct operations in Afghanistan. The joint force would eventually include ground forces from the Special Operations Force, the Army, and the Marine Corps; air power from the

Navy, Air Force, and Marines; support, including space and airborne surveillance, lift, and air refueling—all part of a truly joint effort. The Navy portion of this story follows.

Peleliu immediately sailed from her operations in Australia. As the *Roosevelt* battle group and the *Bataan* ARG sailed from their bases, their families knew they were not saying good-bye for a normal deployment, that these ships were sailing to war. *Bataan* was specially configured for anticipated expeditionary operations in Afghanistan.

Recognizing this was going to be an unusual war, the *Kitty Hawk,* who was forward stationed in Japan, had most of her air wing taken off; Army, Navy, and Air Force special forces embarked with helicopters and equipment prior to departure for the North Arabian Sea. As *Kitty Hawk* closed from the east, *Roosevelt* closed from the west, with *Bataan* close behind.

As the joint force prepared for strikes, P-3 maritime patrol aircraft, joint unmanned vehicles, and Navy carrier-based photoreconnaissance were just a few of the platforms that surveilled Afghanistan. In conjunction with special operations forces on the ground, they were critical to the strike planning.

Coordinated targeting information was turned into actual aim points for weapons loaded on board strike aircraft from *Vinson* and *Enterprise,* as well as Tomahawk cruise missiles and other joint strike assets.

On 7 October, less than a month after the terrorist attack, strikes began with cruise missiles from submarines and surface ships. Strike aircraft from carriers as well as Air Force bombers destroyed critical command and control nodes, ammunition stores, and air defense systems as U.S. and coalition forces "terrorized the terrorists."

Special operations forces on the ground were able to electronically target hidden enemy forces and transmit the information via satellite to the carriers and regional command centers. These data enabled time-critical strikes to be made against elusive targets by carrier-based attack aircraft and Air Force bombers.

These strikes continued over the next few weeks. In only five weeks, these strikes led to the fall of Mazar-e-Sharif, Herat, Jalalabad, and Kabul.

It became clear that there was a need to demonstrate U.S. resolve by committing conventional American ground troops. With the arrival of *Bataan,* the expeditionary force reached critical mass. Navy SEALs were put on the ground near Kandahar in preparation for expeditionary operations with Marines.

Air Force aircraft airlifted Marines from their bases in the United States to a staging base in-theater. From that land base they moved to the sea base, where they joined other Marines and embarked equipment. From the sea base, supported by Marine attack helicopters and Marine and Navy attack aircraft, they moved to the area south of Kandahar, to establish Camp Rhino. Navy Seabees were on the ground within days, preparing the runways and infrastructure necessary for an extended stay by Marines and coalition forces.

Overall, this decisive joint campaign was virtually over in just two months. Humanitarian assistance was part of the operation throughout. *Enterprise,* who conducted strikes for the first few weeks, returned home as the campaign ended, continuing the Navy rotational cycle.

This war was a precision strike war in a land-locked country. If Afghanistan were transposed over the United States, it would have been the equivalent of conducting strikes from the Gulf of Mexico to Chicago. The strikes demonstrated the enduring value of sovereign naval power. The statistics of the naval contribution to the total joint effort bear this out.

But naval forces did more than conduct air strikes. The expeditionary strike conducted by the Marines was farther inland than any previous landings conducted by the U.S. Marine Corps. It was a key to the breaking of the Kandahar stalemate.

Without doubt, this was a special operations war. Navy SEALs and their joint partners conducted a full range of operations, from surveillance and targeting to maritime interdiction and antiterrorist training. Special operations forces were the center of gravity of the ground campaign.

It was also a coalition operation. Many allied partners can contribute ships much more readily than land forces. Remember that a carrier battle group is six to ten U.S. ships, but this is multiplied when coalition ships are considered. Coalition surface forces, as well as aircraft—particularly air refueling tankers—were a critical part of our success.

Sustaining and supporting the effort was an entire Navy team that doesn't show up on the front page. While the fight was on, here are some of the things the Navy did.

The Navy logistics force performed superbly, supplying the equivalent of the city of Sarasota, Florida, in the North Arabian Sea. Medical personnel and facilities in Navy ships were used to provide medical support to our Afghan partners. Navy SEALS on the ground helped provide critical humanitarian assistance. Navy Explosive Ordnance Disposal teams provided ordnance disposal support throughout Afghanistan.

In Guantánamo Bay, Navy Seabees prepared Camp X-ray for the arrival of al-Qaeda and Taliban detainees, with Marines providing critical security forces. Navy patrol craft operated under the Coast Guard to secure our maritime boarders. Navy SEALs were part of a joint special forces team ordered to the Philippines to train Filipino forces in combating terrorists. Maritime interdiction operations were conducted worldwide to counter the al-Qaeda maritime network.

Nimitz, fresh from an overhaul, conducted coalition-building exercises with South American navies. The *Bon Homme Richard* amphibious group was able to provide critical humanitarian assistance in Kenya en route to its deployment. Forces continued to deploy to Europe to reassure and train with our NATO partners. *Essex* provided stabilization to the crisis in East Timor.

A final joint story revolves around the air base in Diego Garcia. The Navy destroyer USS *Russell* was assigned to provide air defense, and when a B-1 crashed after takeoff, the ship was able to quickly rescue the pilots and return them to their base.

Although the Navy conducted all of these operations as part of a joint team, Operation Enduring Freedom highlighted the value of sovereign, forward, and immediately employable naval forces. And today, the Navy is still out there . . . arrayed across the world . . . ready to respond to the next crisis . . . anywhere . . . anytime.

U.S. Navy and Coalition Maritime Operations During Operation Iraqi Freedom

3

Lt. Garrett D. Kasper, USN, a 1996 NROTC graduate of Marquette University with a B.A. in public relations, currently serves as the assistant public affairs officer for media operations at Commander, U.S. Naval Forces Central Command/Commander, U.S. Fifth Fleet.

On 19 March 2003, the United States and its coalition partners began Operation Iraqi Freedom, the multinational effort to liberate the people of Iraq from the oppressive regime of Saddam Hussein. Together, the coalition fought to

Find and eliminate Iraq's weapons of mass destruction

Capture terrorists and disestablish suspected terrorist cells

Secure Iraqi oil fields and offshore oil terminals to preserve the environment and guard the Iraqi economy from sabotage

End United Nations sanctions and provide immediate humanitarian assistance

End Saddam Hussein's dictatorship

Help the Iraqi people transition to a nonthreatening, representative form of self-government

Power Projection: Just the Right Amount of Concentrated Naval Forces

During Operation Iraqi Freedom (OIF), five carrier strike groups, three amphibious ready groups, and two amphibious task forces totaling more than 200 coalition ships and more than 77,000 Sailors and embarked Marines were assigned to Commander, Naval Forces Central Command/Commander, U.S. Fifth Fleet (COMNAV-CENT/COMFIFTHFLT). The advancements in communications, strike warfare, and the introduction of the Navy's new F/A-18E/F Super Hornet, combined with our use of special forces and Toma-hawk land-attack missile strikes, allowed the coalition to take Baghdad within three weeks.

More than 780 Navy and Marine Corps aircraft were among the 1,800 total coalition aircraft used in OIF. Naval aircraft from air-craft carriers and large-deck amphibious ships flew nearly 14,000 sorties in support of OIF, averaging 1,500 sorties per day. USS *Abraham Lincoln* (CVN 72), USS *Constellation* (CV 64,) and USS *Kitty Hawk* (CV 63) carrier strike groups (CSG) conducted opera-tions from the Arabian Gulf, while USS *Harry S. Truman* (CVN 75) and USS *Theodore Roosevelt* (CVN 71) operated from the U.S. Sixth Fleet's waters in the Mediterranean. All five CSGs were under the operational control of COMNAVCENT/COMFIFTHFLT.

OIF Sortie Statistics from 19 March–21 April 2003

Average number of Navy combatant sorties per day (34 days): 152

Average number of Navy combatant sorties per week (4.9 weeks): 1,055

Average number of Navy support sorties per day (34 days): 82

Average number of Navy support sorties per week (4.9 weeks): 565

Average number of Navy sorties per day (34 days): 234

Average number of Navy sorties per week (4.9 weeks): 1,620

Highest number of Navy sorties: 425; 269 [63 percent] combat-ant and 156 [37 percent] support on 2 April

A New F/A-18: The Super Hornet Adds More Sting During Combat

F/A-18E and F/A-18F Super Hornets, with sophisticated elec-tronic, payload, and range improvements, were deployed in com-bat for the first time aboard USS *Abraham Lincoln* (CVN 72) and USS *Nimitz* (CVN 68). The inaugural Super Hornet squadron, VFA-115, was deployed aboard *Lincoln,* while VFA-14 and VFA-41 were part of Carrier Air Wing 11 on *Nimitz.* In early April, two

F/A-18Es from VFA-14 and two F/A-18Fs from VFA-41 flew 4,000 miles ahead of *Nimitz,* landing aboard *Lincoln* to augment Carrier Air Wing 14.

The addition of four Super Hornets aboard *Lincoln* provided a flexible mix of fighter support and tanker capability to support coalition forces on the ground in Iraq. A unique aspect of OIF was the mid-mission adaptability of carrier-based strike aircraft. Traditionally, pilots would take off with a pre-scripted set of targets and return to the carrier once their ordnance was expended. During OIF, the process of determining targets, from mission planning to target engagement, was measured in hours instead of days or weeks. This ability, combined with the Super Hornet's ability to carry more ordnance and stay in the air longer, allowed for the mid-mission exploitation of pop-up targets. Fewer flights were required, putting fewer pilots in harm's way and leading, overall, to a more decisive air campaign.

Advanced Weaponry: Technology Aids Flexibility and Accuracy

More than 800 Tomahawk land-attack missiles (TLAMs) were fired from thirty-five coalition ships, one-third of which were submarines, between 19 March and 3 April 2003. With new technological advancements in the TLAM program, there was a dramatic reduction in the time required between acquiring a target and launching a missile. Missions used to take days to plan, but now they take just a few hours, allowing TLAMs to be programmed with the freshest intelligence and mitigating unintended collateral damage.

More than 75 percent of Navy aircraft used in OIF employed Joint-Directed Attack Munitions (JDAMs), which are essentially traditional "dumb-bombs" outfitted with a satellite-guided navigation system, which automatically corrects its flight path during deployment for maximum accuracy. With JDAMs aboard naval aircraft, pilots were able to attack many more "targets of opportunity" during their missions with unparalleled accuracy and without wasting ordnance.

On 21 March, thirty U.S. Navy and coalition warships launched more than 380 TLAMs against significant, real-time military targets of interest. The U.S. ships that launched Tomahawks were: *Bunker Hill* (CG 52), *Mobile Bay* (CG 53), *San Jacinto* (CG 56), *Cowpens* (CG 63), *Shiloh* (CG 67), *Briscoe* (DD 977), *Deyo*

(DD 989), *Fletcher* (DD 992), *Arleigh Burke* (DDG 51), *John S. McCain* (DDG 56), *Paul Hamilton* (DDG 60), *Milius* (DDG 69), *Higgins* (DDG 71), *Donald Cook* (DDG 75), *O'Kane* (DDG 77), *Porter* (DDG 78), *Oscar Austin* (DDG 79), *Augusta* (SSN 710), *Providence* (SSN 719), *Pittsburgh* (SSN 720), *Key West* (SSN 722), *Louisville* (SSN 724), *Newport News* (SSN 750), *San Juan* (SSN 751), *Boise* (SSN 764), *Montpelier* (SSN 765), *Toledo* (SSN 769), *Columbia* (SSN 771), and *Cheyenne* (SSN 773). They were joined by two Royal Navy submarines, HMS *Splendid* and HMS *Turbulent*.

Aegis Weapons System: A New Use for the Fleet's Shield

In addition to their strike, surface, subsurface, electronic, and air warfare capabilities, certain Aegis-equipped U.S. Navy guided-missile cruisers and destroyers performed the ballistic missile defense role with their highly sensitive phased-array radar suite. This defense system allowed naval units to provide early warning and detection, and transmit real-time data with the land-based Patriot missile batteries for engagement. The ballistic missile defense system successfully engaged thirteen missiles, with naval units providing early warning and detection in twelve of those engagements.

Submarine Force: Silent Flexibility Leads to Unprecedented Successes

COMNAVCENT/COMFIFTHFLT more than doubled the record of submarines operating in this area of responsibility during OIF, by overseeing an unprecedented fifteen submarines in the AOR simultaneously. The previous record was set during Operation Enduring Freedom, when the maximum number of submarines allocated to the region was six. The fifteen subs included twelve U.S. submarines, two British Tomahawk shooters, and one Danish submarine that provided information and warning capabilities.

The submarine force's ability to reposition at high speed proved to be invaluable. Within days of Turkey's denial of overland flight privileges for coalition air assets, submarines surged from the Mediterranean Sea expeditiously to the Fifth Fleet region. The submarine assets were seamlessly integrated and resupplied at sea with ships from Commander, Task Force 53.

Naval Special Warfare: Stealth and Flexibility

In the first hours of OIF, Navy SEALS, joined by British Royal Marines, raided two massive gas and oil platforms (GOPLATs) in the Arabian Gulf, just off the Iraqi coast. Fifteen Iraqi soldiers were captured, along with a cache of grenade launchers, AK-47s, and surface-to-air missiles.

Securing the platforms from Iraqi enemy forces was a priority for the coalition. Before the war, 80 percent of Iraq's oil flowed through the two forty-eight-inch pipelines from the Al-Faw Peninsula, to the platforms, and directly into the holds of supertankers. If enemy forces had succeeded in destroying these two platforms (Khor al-Amaya and Mina al-Bakr), not only would the Iraqi people have lost significant oil revenues, but also the potential environmental damage would have been catastrophic. The amount of oil that could have been spilled from the terminals would have equaled an Exxon *Valdez*–type oil spill every two hours.

Using Rigid Hull Inflatable Boats (RHIBs) and Mark V boats, U.S. Navy SEALs cleared, surveyed, and provided security for both the Khawr Abd Allah (KAA) and Khaw al Zubayr (KAZ) waterways, as well as the entire al-Faw Peninsula in southern Iraq. Securing the KAA was especially important in facilitating later delivery of humanitarian supplies to the people of Umm Qasr and Basrah in southern Iraq.

The SEALs used the HSV-X1 *Joint Venture*—an aluminum-hulled catamaran ferry modified to carry gunboats, amphibious landing craft, helicopters, and Marine platoons—as their forward operating base while operating in the vicinity of Umm Qasr. *Joint Venture* provided supplies, shelter, and spare parts for more than a dozen SEAL boats operating in the KAA and KAZ waterways. Without the *Joint Venture,* SEALs would have had to travel hundreds of miles to reach bases in Kuwait for fuel and supplies, greatly reducing time on station, as well as the waiting time for humanitarian supplies.

U.S. Coast Guard: Same Mission, Just Overseas

U.S. Coast Guard forces played a small but significant role during OIF. Although serving in support of the Department of Defense is nothing new for the Coast Guard, OIF saw the largest deployment of Coast Guard forces to a combat theater in thirty years.

Prior to the commencement of combat operations, Coast Guard cutters participated in MIOs. They worked in concert with coalition naval forces to enforce United Nations sanctions that proscribed the sale of Iraqi oil, except as allowed under the "Oil-for-Food" program. During MIOs, the Coast Guard Cutter *Boutwell* utilized her over-the-horizon rigid hull inflatable boat and three boarding teams to board and inspect numerous vessels bound for and departing the Iraqi port of Umm Qasr.

When combat operations commenced, Coast Guard cutters provided security for the assault to seize and secure two massive Iraqi offshore oil terminals. Once the terminals were safely in coalition hands, detachments from two Coast Guard port security units, PSU 311 and PSU 313, went aboard to maintain security and protect them until combat operations were complete and the terminals could be returned to civilian control. As soon as coalition forces had secured the Iraqi port of Umm Qasr, elements of PSU 311 deployed there to provide waterside security. The port security units also maintained security at two ports in Kuwait and were joined in that effort by PSU 309.

The Coast Guard Cutter (CGC) *Aquidneck,* a 110-foot patrol boat, was the first coalition vessel to arrive on scene following the tragic mid-air collision of two coalition helicopters; the cutter's crew assumed the role of on-scene commander.

Coast Guard 110-foot patrol boats also played significant roles during operations on the KAA waterway. After the oil terminals were secured, the patrol boats provided flank security for the amphibious assault across the waterway by British forces to seize Iraq's al-Faw Peninsula. During this operation, CGC *Adak* rescued three Iraqi sailors from the water and took them into custody as prisoners of war. *Adak* also assisted with the capture of Iraqi mine-laying vessels, preventing the release of dozens of Iraqi mines.

The patrol boats also provided security for coalition warships engaged in naval gunfire support for coalition troops on al-Faw. The patrol boats then provided security for coalition mine-clearing operations on the KAA, often operating ahead of minesweepers in uncleared waters. When the waterway was sufficiently cleared of mines, the patrol boats escorted vessels transporting humanitarian aid to the Iraqi people.

CGC *Walnut,* a 225-foot buoy tender, deployed to the Arabian Gulf along with personnel from the Coast Guard National Strike Team to fight maritime oil pollution in anticipation of environmental warfare by the Saddam Hussein regime. Fortunately, those capabilities were not needed, and *Walnut* was pressed into service reestablishing the long-neglected system of aids to navigation on the KAA in preparation for the resumption of normal waterborne commerce.

Following combat operations, the 110-foot patrol boats continued to patrol the KAA to prevent piracy, regulate the flow of traffic, and foster the resumption of normal commerce. They continue to patrol, providing safety, security, and stability to help the people of Iraq reestablish maritime trade and commerce.

Mine Warfare and Explosive Ordnance Disposal: Eliminating the Hidden Threat

The mine warfare mission was one of Naval Forces Central (NAVCENT)'s efforts during OIF. With a team of four U.S. and five coalition minesweepers, plus five mine-countermeasure helicopters, Explosive Ordnance Disposal (EOD) teams were able to clear 913 nautical miles of water in the KAA and Umm Qasr waterways. More than 230 mine-like objects were detected; 90 mines were found, 11 of which were destroyed. Five of those mines destroyed were ultrasensitive Italian-made Manta mines uncovered at low tide. They were clearly deployed in a hasty manner by the Iraqis and fortunately not deep enough to threaten large ships. EOD also cleared twenty-one berths and all land areas in new and old ports.

The Marine Mammal System (MMS)'s bottlenose dolphins were absolutely invaluable to the success of mine-clearance operations in the KAA and Umm Qasr waterways. Through teamwork and ingenuity, the mammals were airlifted to pools on the beach and were then dispatched to clear mines in shallow and silted waterways with their superior biological sensory sonar. In another unprecedented instance, the mammals were pooled in large tanks in the well deck aboard USS *Gunston Hall* (LSD 5).

Numerous mine-like objects were discovered by MMS and unmanned underwater vehicles, which streamlined the identification process of questionable items. Instead of wasting valuable time underwater with divers, debris such as car tires and fifty-gallon drums could be identified and ignored.

EOD teams in the waterways near Umm Qasr cleared twenty-one berths in the port to ensure the safe navigation of all humanitarian aid shipments. EOD teams disposed of more than 4,900 items for a total net explosive weight of almost 36,000 pounds of unexploded and stockpiled ordnance. Coalition divers conducted a total of 174 dives for a total bottom time of more than 110 hours. U.S. Navy EOD teams assigned to the Marine Corps Engineering Group on the ground disposed of more than 800,000 items for a total net explosive weight of more than 330,000 pounds of unexploded and stockpiled ordnance.

Navy EOD teams on land worked together to clear twenty-seven weapons caches, twenty-four neighborhoods, a train station, and a hospital. They also played an integral role in the preservation of Iraqi oil wells from sabotage by the Iraqi regime. More than 400 Iraqi oil wells were cleared, resulting in the disposal of more than twenty weapons and ammunition caches with a net explosive weight of almost 11,000 pounds.

EOD teams also conducted salvage and recovery operations in support of U.S. and coalition aircraft downed during OIF. They recovered two Royal Navy SH-3 helicopters and seven dead air crewmen, a Marine A/V-8B Harrier near Kuwait, and an F/A-18 and its deceased pilot near Karbala. They also scuttled two partially submerged dhows (hazards to navigation) and salvaged two sunken patrol boats in Umm Qasr and Kor Azubahr.

EOD units continue to support OIF by identifying and destroying unexploded ordnance in Baghdad and throughout Iraq.

A Global War: Coalition of the Willing Contributions

During OIF, coalition forces provided integral support to the NAVCENT theater. Along with the presence of U.S. and British warships, naval units from the Spanish, Danish, Polish, Australian, Emirati, Bahraini, and Kuwaiti navies made significant contributions to the overall operation. Naval assets from seventeen nations conducted more than 5,600 ship queries and more than 1,100 boardings in support of the global War on Terrorism. Additionally, more than 415 ships were safely escorted through both the Bab Al Mendeb Straits and the Strait of Hormuz.

A Spanish flotilla of three ships and 900 personnel departed Spain in March and arrived in the northern Arabian Gulf on 8 April. The next day, the amphibious landing ship *Galicia* sailed up the KAA waterway to Umm Qasr and off-loaded a forty-bed field hospital with fifty-three medical personnel, a biological and chemical decontamination team, and a construction battalion.

SPS *Galicia* off-loaded more than 20 tons of humanitarian aid cargo in Umm Qasr, including 29,000 Muslim rations, 8 tons of bottled fresh water, 10,000 blankets, 30 large tents, and a complete desalinization plant.

The government of Japan has contributed in excess of 86,629,675 gallons of F76 fuel—worth more than 76 million dollars—since the inception of Operation Enduring Freedom.

The crew of Canadian Operation Enduring Freedom asset HMCS *Montreal* boarded a ship off the coast of the United Arab Emirates, which resulted in the detention of seven Iraqi nationals who had in their possession two gas masks, forty vials of atropine, a decontamination kit, and materials for making Molotov cocktails. The suspected vessel did not have navigational materials or records of any kind.

The Gulf Cooperation Council established the Kuwaiti Defense Force/Peninsula Shield to help protect Kuwait in the event of an Iraqi invasion. The maritime portion of this force was comprised of fifteen combatant vessels from Bahrain, United Arab Emirates, and Kuwait. These forces were instrumental in supporting maritime interception operations, protecting seaports of debarkation, and providing sea lines of communication and security. Never before in history has an armada of this caliber been built. The technological innovation, speed, and lethality of coalition naval forces constricted the Iraqi regime early, allowing forces to advance to Baghdad in an astonishing three weeks.

Conclusion

Whether planning and launching TLAMs, flying sorties, diverting oil smugglers, disabling enemy ordnance, healing the wounded, or rebuilding a war-torn nation, the U.S. Navy's Sailors and Marines assigned to the NAVCENT/COMFIFTHFLT theater played a vital role in world history through their training, skill, and dedication to freedom for everyone.

Military Sealift Command Operations in Enduring Freedom and Iraqi Freedom   4

MSC Operations in Enduring Freedom and Iraqi Freedom

Vice Adm. David L. Brewer III, USN, is commander, Military Sealift Command (MSC), in Washington, D.C. Admiral Brewer's distinguished naval career began on 17 May 1970, when he was commissioned an ensign in the U.S. Navy by former Secretary of the Navy Sen. John Chafee (Rhode Island). He was a member of the first graduating class of the first naval ROTC unit at a historically black university, Prairie View A&M University, Prairie View, Texas.

MSC provides ocean transportation services for the Department of Defense both in peacetime and in war.

War may be obvious, but peacetime missions include more than just the resupply of overseas bases. Our missions can and have included humanitarian missions for disaster relief from hurricanes and other natural disasters, as well as assistance with manmade disasters.

The MSC mission requires a worldwide organization and a global workforce. Headquartered in Washington, D.C., MSC has area commands in Norfolk, Virginia; San Diego, California; Naples, Italy; Manama, Bahrain; and Yokohama, Japan.

Our five area commands coordinate regional requirements for MSC ships in support of the Navy's numbered fleets and geographic commanders. Each MSC area commander is integrated into, and reports operationally to, the commander of MSC via the chain of command of a numbered fleet commander.

Global Workforce

Today, MSC has more than 8,000 employees.

Nearly 80 percent of our people serve at sea. We're working to change that to 90 percent by realigning our shore-side structure and eliminating redundancies. MSC is the single largest employer of merchant mariners in the United States, with currently more than 4,100 U.S. civil service mariners and more than 2,100 commercial mariners working for ship operating companies under contract to MSC.

MSC also has access to more than 1,400 selected Navy reservists. They provide cargo afloat rig teams for underway replenishment to the fleet, seaport operations personnel, and individuals to supplement command center operations in the high-operating-tempo environment that accompanies war or contingency operations.

National Security Roles

MSC strategically prepositions combat cargo for the U.S. Marine Corps, Air Force, Army, and Navy around the world and conducts resupply missions to such out-of-the-way places as McMurdo Sound in Antarctica and Thule Air Base in Greenland. If U.S. forces participate in an international exercise anywhere around the globe, MSC delivers the combat equipment and supplies the ground forces' needs, just as would happen in a war or contingency. In a major theater of war, 95 percent of the war fighters' combat equipment and supplies are delivered by sea.

MSC History

MSC began as the Military Sea Transportation Service, or MSTS, in 1949. World War II had demonstrated the critical need for a consolidated and better-organized system of ocean transportation. During the war, sealift had been handled by four completely different organizations: the Navy and the Army Transportation Services, the War Shipping Administration, and the Fleet Service Forces. The result, at times, was total confusion.

MSTS received its first 209 ships from the Navy and the Army Transportation Services.

The first test of the new command was a trial by fire in Korea, where MSTS moved 99.6 percent of all cargo and 86 percent of the United Nations personnel transported to Korea. In this first major conflict of the Cold War era, MSTS transported 22 million tons of fuel and 54 million tons of dry cargo.

The war in Vietnam was the second major test of sealift capability. At the peak of the war, the command controlled 436 ships and delivered nearly 90 million tons of weapons, ammunition, food, and supplies and more than 20 million tons of fuel to the Southeast Asia theater of operations.

In the 1960s MSTS also began to take on new and different roles. MSTS ships began conducting special missions to support oceanographic research, missile tracking, and communications. Then undersea surveillance missions and support of deep submergence vessels were added. In 1970 the MSTS name was changed to Military Sealift Command, and a new mission was added; namely, fleet combat logistics—providing fuel, supplies, and support to Navy fleets.

MSC has been involved in world events ever since: Vietnam, the Gulf War, Somalia, the Balkans, Haiti, Bosnia-Herzegovina, Kosovo, Operation Iraqi Freedom (OIF), and the global War on Terrorism.

U.S. Merchant Mariner

America's merchant mariners have sailed into harm's way for the nation since 1775. In 1898 the U.S. fleet that carried out the Cuban invasion with Teddy Roosevelt consisted of seventeen chartered ships and two purchased steamers. The crews were merchant mariners.

World War II saw some of the most horrific sea battles the world had ever known. In fact, more than 700 merchant ships were lost in World War II, and more than 6,000 merchant mariners died as a result of enemy action. Only the U.S. Marine Corps had a higher mortality rate in that war.

In the early 1950s, commercial merchant mariners formed the backbone of the sealift "bridge of ships" across the Pacific as the United States moved to defend against Communism in Korea.

In 1968 alone, merchant mariners sailing with the MSTS lifted 19 million tons of cargo to Vietnam for the U.S. Army.

During Operations Desert Shield and Desert Storm in 1990, merchant mariners sailed in more than 250 ships that formed a "bridge of steel" from the East Coast of the United States to the Middle East, with literally one ship every fifty miles. During OIF in 2003, these great Americans sailed in more than 200 ships, again building a bridge, the "steel bridge of democracy," to liberate the people of Iraq.

Business Lines

Today MSC operates four business lines, or programs, to meet the diverse needs of its many and varied customers. The programs are the Naval Fleet Auxiliary Force, Special Mission Program, Prepositioning Program, and Sealift Program.

Naval Fleet Auxiliary Force

MSC's thirty-six Naval Fleet Auxiliary Force (NFAF) ships are the lifelines to U.S. Navy ships at sea. Providing fuel, food, ammunition, spare parts, and other supplies, these ships enable the Navy fleet to work at the highest operational tempo possible, alleviating the need for the combatants to constantly return to port for supplies or refueling. MSC ships conduct underway resupply missions as connected replenishments and/or as vertical replenishments via helicopter.

NFAF ships include fleet oilers, combat stores ships, fast combat support ships, ammunition ships, hospital ships, and fleet ocean tugs. A new class of dry cargo/ammunition ships, the *Lewis and Clark*–class (T-AKE), will begin joining the MSC fleet in 2005 to replace aging ammunition and combat stores ships.

NFAF ships are crewed by federal civil service mariners, with small Navy departments aboard some ships for supply and aviation functions.

Special Mission Program

MSC's Special Mission Program provides twenty-two ships as platforms for a variety of missions for the Navy and the Department of Defense (DoD), including oceanographic survey, undersea surveillance, submarine support, missile range instrumentation, cable laying and repair, acoustic survey, navigation testing, and support for Navy SEAL teams.

Oceanographic survey ships help chart ocean bottoms and coastlines. The data they gather provide accurate charts that benefit all maritime users.

Undersea surveillance ships provide direct support to the fleets with information on undersea activity.

Special Mission Program ships are crewed primarily by commercial mariners working for ship operating companies under contract to MSC. Sponsoring organizations provide mission crews for the vessels.

Prepositioning Program

Begun in the early 1980s, MSC's Prepositioning Program is one of the mainstays of U.S. readiness around the world. Prepositioning ships normally are strategically located in three areas: Diego Garcia in the Indian Ocean, Guam/Saipan in the western Pacific, and in the Mediterranean Sea.

Prepositioning ships support the U.S. Marine Corps, Army, Air Force, Navy, and Defense Logistics Agency. The ships forward deploy combat gear, vehicles, supplies, ammunition, and fuel to rapidly support U.S. combat operations wherever needed, whenever required.

Of the thirty-five Afloat Prepositioning Force ships, sixteen are government owned and nineteen are long-term commercial charters. All are crewed by contract mariners working for ship operating companies under contract to MSC.

Sealift Program

MSC's Sealift Program deploys and redeploys U.S. military combat vehicles, equipment, and supplies wherever needed using both government-owned ships and commercial charters. The program charters commercial vessels for time and/or voyage use. All operate under MSC control as part of the U.S. Transportation Command.

The Military Sealift Program provides a flexible force. It can be expanded dramatically in times of national crisis by chartering additional private industry ships or activating government-owned assets from reduced operating status. During OIF, the Military Sealift Program had as many as 127 ships under its control or under charter.

In peacetime, private sector ships transport military equipment and petroleum products point to point for requirements not serviced by regularly scheduled liner service. When commercial industry ships cannot meet cargo/delivery requirements (e.g., heavy, bulky, outsized equipment), government-owned sealift assets may be used.

MSC also maintains a surge sealift fleet in reduced operating status. This consists of eight fast sealift ships and eleven large, medium-speed roll-on/roll-off ships, or LMSRs. In addition, MSC has access to the Ready Reserve Force (RRF): sixty-eight militarily useful ships owned and maintained by the U.S. Maritime Administration (MARAD), part of the U.S. Department of Transportation. When RRF ships are activated, they come under MSC's operational control.

Operation Enduring Freedom

Since the beginning of the global War on Terrorism, MSC has been at the forefront of U.S. efforts, providing a variety of innovative services and huge amounts of combat supplies to U.S. and allied forces around the world.

In addition to overseas support, USNS *Comfort*, one of MSC's two 894-foot, 1,000-bed hospital ships, was activated immediately after the terrorist attacks on September 11, 2001. *Comfort* sailed to New York City to provide much-needed on-site relief for rescue and emergency personnel working around the clock in harsh conditions at Ground Zero, the site of the World Trade Center attack.

Comfort served 17,000 meals for 6,650 guests/relief workers, processed more than 4,000 pounds of laundry, and conducted 561 medical consults.

In the early stages of Operation Enduring Freedom, the MSC Afloat Prepositioning Force was also called into action. Prepositioning ship MV *Maj. Bernard F. Fisher* delivered 373 twenty-foot containers of U.S. Air Force munitions to Diego Garcia for Air Force planes participating in the operation.

Maritime Prepositioning ship SS *Maj. Stephen W. Pless* was called into action when Taliban and al-Qaeda detainees under U.S. control were flown to the U.S. naval base at Guantánamo Bay, Cuba. This ship normally prepositions Marine Corps equipment and supplies in the Mediterranean Sea, but was in Norfolk, Virginia, completing routine maintenance when the call came to assist Joint

Task Force 160. With very little advance notice, *Pless* was able to transport a fleet hospital and more than sixty support vehicles to Guantánamo.

Cargo Moved for Operation Enduring Freedom

Since September 11, 2001, MSC has moved 22.8 million square feet of vehicles, aircraft, and rolling stock, primarily into the Middle East, for the global War on Terrorism.

Nineteen million square feet moved via U.S. flag shipping. Of this, 17.6 million square feet moved via government-owned ships; the remainder was moved by commercial charter.

Foreign-flag ships moved only about 3.8 million square feet.

Operation Iraqi Freedom

Following the first Gulf War, the U.S. Army began positioning combat equipment and supplies ashore in Kuwait for periodic combined U.S.–Kuwaiti military exercises. In July 2002 USNS *Watkins*, an LMSR used to preposition Army combat gear at Diego Garcia in the Indian Ocean, off-loaded her cargo in Kuwait for Exercise Vigilant Hammer. This time, however, there was no backload of the cargo. It was left ashore. This may, perhaps, have been the first indication of the impending Operation Iraqi Freedom.

In early October 2002, an MSC commercial charter carried vehicles and rolling stock for the Army's Third Infantry Division to Southwest Asia. Later that month two more prepositioning ships delivered their mission cargoes. MV *Capt. Steven L. Bennett* off-loaded Air Force munitions at Diego Garcia, and USNS *Watson* off-loaded Army combat gear in Kuwait for Exercise Vigilant Python.

December saw additional Army gear deployed to Kuwait for Exercise Desert Spring, continuing the pattern of no backloads.

Then, in January 2003, the buildup began in earnest for what would become Operation Iraqi Freedom. MSC was helping reposition U.S. military forces to support the president's campaign against terrorism. Naval Fleet Auxiliary Force combat logistics ships were working at an increased operational tempo to support carrier battle groups and amphibious ready groups that were repositioning to Southwest Asia. In early January, hospital ship USNS *Comfort* deployed.

From January through the end of April, MSC moved more than 21 million square feet of war-fighting cargo and equipment for the Army, Marine Corps, Air Force, and Navy in support of OIF.

At the same time, MSC ships carried more than 261 million gallons of fuel for Army, Marine Corps, and Air Force war fighters and pumped more than 117 million gallons of ship and aircraft fuel to Navy combat ships around the world. Altogether, MSC moved more than one-third of a billion gallons of fuel.

Force Protection Challenges

As the buildup for OIF began in January, force protection teams from primarily the Army and Marine Corps provided shipboard security and protection from terrorists aboard MSC ships. The first fleet force protection team was from the I Marine Expeditionary Force (MEF) and reported aboard 24 January 2002. This employment was an interim solution for force protection until the Guardian Mariner Program came into full operation.

Under the Guardian Mariner Program, more than 1,300 Army National Guard troops were activated to provide force protection and security aboard MSC ships sailing to and from Southwest Asia. The soldiers, from Puerto Rico National Guard Unit 92d Separate Infantry Brigade, were organized into 110 twelve-person teams. They began reporting aboard MSC ships in mid-March.

In all, about seventy fleet force protection teams and seventy-five Guardian Mariner teams were used aboard MSC ships during OIF.

Desert Storm versus Iraqi Freedom

For MSC there was a significant difference between Operations Desert Storm and Iraqi Freedom.

When Iraq invaded Kuwait in August 1990, MSC had twenty-four ships in the Prepositioning Program, predominantly for the Marine Corps. The Marines had begun prepositioning combat gear around the world in the early 1980s.

The average capacity of each of the twenty-four prepositioning ships used in Desert Storm was 50,000 square feet, and their average speed was thirteen knots.

At that time the Army was committed to Europe and defense against the Warsaw Pact. With the fall of the Berlin Wall and in light of the first Gulf War, the Army's mission changed to a more global focus. That change required additional capacity and capability in the MSC prepositioning fleet for Army combat gear and for Army surge capabilities.

Today, we have thirty-five active ships in the Prepositioning Program that strategically place combat cargo for all services at sea. Eight are LMSRs that came to MSC as a direct result of lessons learned in the first Gulf War. They provide 2 million square feet capacity. Thus, the Prepositioning Program fleet now has more capacity and is faster, averaging seventeen knots during OIF.

We have eleven more LMSRs in our Sealift Program that provide 3 million square feet of new capacity to surge combat equipment from the United States to a theater of operations.

LMSRs are the largest ships in the MSC fleet. They have an average capacity per ship of 300,000 square feet and travel at a maximum speed of twenty-four knots. They are roll-on/roll-off capable, which means you can load the vehicles and rolling stock for an Army heavy armor brigade in just three to four days. Their interconnected decks and large, twin-pedestal cranes for bulky pieces of cargo make this possible.

U.S.- versus Foreign-Flag Charters

In the first Gulf War, we relied heavily on foreign-flagged charters to move the equipment our customers needed because of the lack of prepositioning and surge capacity. For Iraqi Freedom, the trend was reversed.

By the end of the first Gulf War, we had chartered 314 ships: 215 were foreign flag; the others were U.S.-flagged ships and included our government-owned ships and commercial long-term charters in the Prepositioning Program. Almost all of the foreign-flagged chartered ships were used for only one voyage.

For OIF, we used fewer ships overall and fewer foreign-flag voyages than U.S.-flag voyages: forty-three foreign versus seventy-seven U.S., which still included our long-term charters in the Prepositioning Program.

We used fewer commercial ships for two reasons. There was an organized buildup of combat gear in theater during Operation Enduring Freedom, and we employed the incredible 300,000 square-foot capacity of the LMSRs, which resulted in fewer voyages overall because of higher speeds, increased capacity, and faster off-loads.

Lessons Learned from the First Gulf War

MSC learned and applied many lessons from the 1990–1991 Gulf War.

MSC needed and received nineteen LMSRs, which significantly expanded its prepositioning and surge-sealift capacity. In addition, MARAD began upgrading the RRF as a result of lessons learned. MARAD obtained newer, larger, diesel-powered roll-on/roll-off ships to replace World War II–era ships. These newer ships were also kept in a higher state of readiness than prior to the war—making them that much more responsive to activation and more reliable during transits.

Several RRF roll-on/roll-off ships had new spar decks installed to increase the square footage they could carry per load. The spar deck is an added deck welded to the weather deck of the ship. The modification added a new level of efficiency to the RRF.

Efficiency also meant containerization. Containers are easier to handle than open pallets, or break-bulk cargo, resulting in an exponential decrease in on- and off-load time.

Size Does Make a Difference

As stated earlier, one of the key lessons we learned in the first Gulf War led to the addition of nineteen LMSRs to our prepositioning and surge fleets.

Size does make a difference. You can fit 1,000 Bradley fighting vehicles into a single LMSR, whereas it would take almost 240 C-17 Globemaster III or 140 older, but bigger, C-5 Galaxy aircraft to carry the same square footage of combat gear and equipment. While the aircraft fly much faster than LMSRs sail, through prepositioning, MSC can actually get large amounts of the Army's gear to the soldiers who need it, faster and more efficiently, freeing airborne assets for more-immediate and time-critical missions.

Lessons Learned from Operation Iraqi Freedom

The first lesson learned from OIF is confirmation of the lesson we learned in the first Gulf War and validation of the fix: prepositioning works! The prepositioning ships were, once again, first on the scene with significant amounts of combat gear for ground troops. All four services are looking at expansion of their prepositioning efforts as a way to ensure rapid delivery of critical combat cargo to any theater worldwide.

Second, LMSRs performed exactly as they were designed to do. They provided optimum lift with their large capacities and high readiness rate.

Now, we need to expand that capability with purpose-designed, high-speed, shallow-draft vessels that can operate in the littorals and provide faster, more-efficient transport of combat gear from factory to foxhole.

Another lesson we learned in OIF was that up-front funding from the Army allowed uninterrupted support for commercial chartering and activation of government-owned surge ships.

We also relearned the importance of commercial charters. The commercial market was able to cover spikes in demand that could not be met by government-owned ships, so a combination of U.S.- and foreign-flag shipping was used. The MSC chartering/contracting process gave U.S. forces timely, cost-effective sealift.

MSC's Future

As MSC moves into the twenty-first century, our hallmark continues to be innovation through transformation. We're improving customer service and aligning ourselves to be the best-value ocean transporter for the DoD.

Here is a quick look at some of our future projects.

USNS *Supply*/USS *Coronado*

In 2001 MSC took a significant step forward in customer service when the Navy combatant fleet transferred the fast combat support ship, USS *Supply*, to MSC. The USNS *Supply* was the first of four such ships that would transfer to MSC.

In 2002 USS *Arctic* followed *Supply*'s lead and became a USNS ship.

USS *Rainier* transferred to MSC in 2003, and in 2004 we picked up USS *Bridge*.

With all four of these *Supply*-class ships in place, we can save the Navy more than $76 million annually in operational costs and return a total of almost 2,000 Sailor billets to the fleet.

Another area of potential service is MSC operation of flag or command ships. USS *Coronado* was scheduled to transfer to MSC operation 14 November 2003. MSC civilian mariners are to provide engineering, laundry, galley, navigation, and watch-standing services—essentially a seagoing platform for the Navy command staff aboard. Discussions are under way about MSC assuming operation of the Navy's remaining command ships.

New Combat Logistics Ships
In the next decade, MSC will take delivery of up to eleven new dry cargo/ammunition ships, the *Lewis and Clark* class, to modernize combat fleet logistics.

These new dual-product ships—to be built from the keel up—will replace MSC's *Kilauea*-class ammunition ships and *Mars*- and *Sirius*-class combat stores ships.

National Steel and Shipbuilding Company in San Diego will build the new ships to commercial industry standards. They will have speeds of twenty knots, so they will be able to easily keep up with the fleet.

WestPac Express
The III MEF in the Far East needed a more-efficient way of sending up to 900 troops and their rolling stock and supplies out on training exercises.

The Marines had been using as many as twenty-two airlift missions for troops and separate sealift for equipment, requiring up to fourteen days to get all of their troops and equipment staged at their training areas.

The innovative maritime solution: *WestPac Express*, a high-speed, thirty-plus knots transport ship chartered by MSC on a thirty-six-month contract with Austal Ships of Australia.

The vessel carries up to 900 Marines and their vehicles, rolling stock, and gear to the exercise area in approximately one-third the time and as a unit.

As a result, III MEF's combat readiness has significantly improved.

HSV-2 *Swift*
When the mine-countermeasures command ship, USS *Inchon*, was decommissioned, the Navy asked MSC to offer an interim solution. MSC chartered HSV-2 *Swift*, a high-speed (thirty-plus knots) catamaran, to operate as a test platform to fine-tune high-speed vessel technology and tactics for potential use in the mine warfare community.

Built in Tasmania by INCAT to commercial standards, HSV-2 *Swift* is a bare-boat charter and uses U.S. Navy crews who will transport and launch a variety of small craft and equipment from the vessel to explore possibilities in the mine warfare mission.

Concurrently, this vessel will be used as a demonstration platform for a series of experiments, exercises, and training events for the Naval Warfare Development Command and the U.S. Marine Corps.

Salvage Ships and Submarine Tenders

When the CNO challenged MSC to find innovative and cost-efficient ways to serve the Navy, MSC was already operating the oceangoing fleet tugs, which often work in tandem with salvage ships like USS *Grapple* on salvage missions. Transferring operations to MSC would reduce crew sizes due to the relative experience level of MSC civilian mariners. Also, MSC crews are not hindered by operating tempo restrictions.

MSC could also operate submarine tenders. Essentially, they are just combat logistics ships for submarines, and MSC already operates combat logistics for the surface fleets.

All these ideas will return Navy war-fighting billets to the fleet, enhance the Navy's combat-readiness, and save money for recapitalization.

Afloat Forward Staging Base

As the joint arena becomes the primary focus of U.S. military forces, MSC is involved with the CNO's Sea Power 21 and sea-basing through the development of the Afloat Forward Staging Base (AFSB).

To rapidly and efficiently meet the U.S. Marine Corps' future requirements and to support joint forces' ability to launch combat power from the sea, MSC is exploring a commercial approach to the AFSB, leveraging MSC's experience with the maritime community and industry research and development capability.

The potential AFSB concept uses a 1,400-foot commercial container ship with a 140-foot beam and puts a flight deck on top to launch and recover helicopters and, potentially, short take-off and landing, fixed-wing aircraft. The ship would use modular berthing, feeding, medical, and administrative spaces and would incorporate a selective cargo discharge system, automating supply selection and distribution. These technologies are currently available in the commercial world. We need only put them together to meet future sealift challenges.

MSC Transformation

As the DoD moves into the twenty-first century, Military Sealift Command is transforming from a traditional twentieth-century hierarchical organization into a twenty-first-century network-centric organization.

MSC is taking full advantage of new technologies and new processes, while adopting and adapting practices developed in commercial industry to meet the changing needs of our customers worldwide.

MSC is dedicated to providing innovative solutions to the ocean transportation and distribution challenges of the DoD and the federal government.

When combat supplies, equipment, vehicles, and fuel need to be there—wherever, whenever—MSC delivers!

Medical Capabilities on Target

5

Naval Medicine's Support in Operation Iraqi Freedom

Comdr. William P. Bradley, MSC, USN, is the head of the Medical Resources Programming Branch (N931C), Medical Resources, Plans, and Policy Division, Chief of Naval Operations, Washington, D.C. He holds undergraduate and graduate degrees in business administration.

In support of Operation Iraqi Freedom (OIF), more than 6,400 active and 1,900 reserve Navy medical personnel were deployed or mobilized, at sea or on shore. From the battlefield "grunt" corpsmen to the forward resuscitative surgery system (FRSS), the fleet hospitals (FHs), the USNS *Comfort,* and the National Naval Medical Center (NNMC), Bethesda, Maryland, wounded, injured, and ill coalition force warriors, Iraqi prisoners of war, and Iraqi civilians (displaced persons) received the highest quality medical care.

What It Takes to Be Ready When the Bell Rings

Naval wartime medical response capabilities must be robust enough to ensure an immediate and appropriate response to expected joint force battlefield casualty estimates and weapons of mass destruction threats. Because of the Navy and Marine Corps' forward-deployed, expeditionary warfare roles, naval medicine is our nation's "911" first-responder medical force.

Thankfully, during OIF the high potential casualty estimates projected by combatant commanders did not come to fruition.

Technological advances in body armor, the lack of chemical or biological weapons use, and revolutionary war-fighting tactics were the main contributors to lower-than-planned combat casualty rates. Comprehensive defensive medicine measures and practices were also major contributors to historically low disease/non-battle injury (DNBI) rates.

Naval medicine's performance in support of OIF should be assessed in terms of how well we demonstrated competency in the four core qualities of naval forces:

Decisiveness: well-equipped, organized, and trained personnel capable of bringing decisive effects to bear where it counts

Sustainability: quickly arrive and remain on the scene for extended periods of time

Responsiveness: flexibility to operate at sea and on shore

Agility: creative and tailored force packaging

Naval Medicine Is Aligned for Readiness

After Operation Desert Storm, naval medicine embarked on an extensive effort to better organize and train our wartime-required active and reserve medical force, while at the same time optimizing our peacetime health care benefit mission. Naval medicine developed and implemented a Continental United States (CONUS) readiness infrastructure strategy that aligned specific operational platforms to a single military treatment facility (MTF), along with the active duty and reserve manpower required to perform both wartime and peacetime missions. This readiness alignment strategy provides the MTF commander with the authority and the resources to balance the wartime readiness and peacetime benefit missions.

This new component unit identification code (CUIC) strategy established separate UICs for operational platforms associated with specific MTFs. Personnel are now ordered to the UIC of a specific deployable medical platform rather than the UIC of the associated fixed MTF. Although the assigned personnel work in the fixed MTF on a day-to-day basis, the new CUIC manning system emphasizes the wartime/deployment support role for assigned personnel.

The CUIC effort also defined how specialties and subspecialties should be coded to readily identify training requirements, personnel supporting specific platforms, and MTF backfill personnel for deploying platforms, and to identify shortfalls in specific specialties where either changes to staffing or a suitable substitution can be made. Our transition from peacetime to wartime platforms in support of OIF was extremely efficient, responsive, and well organized because of our readiness alignment efforts.

Agile, Phased Medical Response

Naval medicine exists to support naval and joint combat forces in war, and to maintain and sustain the well-being of the fighting forces during peacetime in preparation for war. Naval medical personnel must be prepared to respond effectively and rapidly to the entire spectrum of military operations. Force health protection is the naval medicine strategy for maintaining healthy and fit warriors, casualty prevention, care, and management, and providing family-centered health care. We accomplish this strategy by forward deploying with Navy and Marine Corps units and by maintaining a CONUS MTF-based power projection force. During OIF, naval medicine augmented and mobilized forces on sea and on shore to provide casualty prevention and care—from the foxhole to the CONUS MTF.

Casualty Receiving and Treatment Ships

As the intensity of the conflict increased, naval medical forces were phased into the area of operation (AO). In early February 2003, 252 medical personnel from Naval Medical Centers San Diego and Portsmouth and Naval Hospital Jacksonville augmented fleet surgical teams deployed on board the USS *Tarawa,* USS *Saipan,* USS *Boxer,* and USS *Kearsarge.* These amphibious assault class ships (LHA/LHD) are designed to provide sea-based resuscitative and surgically intensive care. The ships are manned by sixteen-person fleet surgical teams (FST) capable of operating one operating room and thirteen beds during peacetime operations. During wartime operations, eighty-four medical personnel from CONUS MTFs augment the ship to achieve full operating capability. Once the Marines off-load, the medical personnel transform the platforms into casualty receiving and treatment ships (CRTSs). Typical CRTS medical spaces include four operating rooms and sixty patient beds (fifteen intensive care and forty-five intermediate care). For OIF, sixty-nine CRTS augments were also used to provide tailored host nation support at the Bahrain National Defense Hospital.

Hospital Ships

Comfort received an activation order on 26 December 2002 directing the ship to move to an undisclosed location and prepare the medical treatment facility (MTF) at the 1,000-bed level. The level to which the MTF would be staffed would be decided at a future date. The normal requirement to get under way was increased from five days to ten days, and the load-out of supplies and the embarkation of the 340-person preparation crew took place in Baltimore. On 6 January 2003, *Comfort* got under way and made the transit to the Naval Support Activity (Center), Diego Garcia, arriving on 3 February. While in Diego Garcia, the crew continued to load the constant flow of medical supplies, prepare the medical spaces, and train for a possible combat support mission. From 6 to 7 March 2003, 874 personnel from NNMC Bethesda were flown to Bahrain to bring the ship to full capability prior to the initiation of combat operations.

The majority of the *Comfort* MTF crew was billeted at the NNMC Bethesda, and remained there to continue an intensified training program that included sending a team of trauma/critical care physicians, plastic and reconstructive surgeons, and critical care nurses to Brook Army Medical Center in San Antonio, Texas, for refresher training in burn care. A program initiated at Suburban Hospital in Bethesda, a Level II Trauma Center, allowed nurse corps and hospital corps personnel to obtain some exposure to trauma cases while awaiting their deployment order.

The following list details some of the statistics from the *Comfort* OIF deployment; most of the statistics cover the six-week period from 22 March to 6 May 2003, when the ship was on station in the North Arabian Gulf (NAG).

 Comfort Deployment Workload:
  Outpatient Visits: 5,004
   Ship's Company: 4,701 (Immunizations)

Coalition Forces: 303
Admissions: 364
    Coalition Forces: 166 (WIA: 33)
    Iraqi Citizens
        EPW: 60 (WIA: 60)
        Civilians: 138 (WIA: 123)
Surgical Procedures: 648 (588 30-day)
Blood Transfusions: 509 pRBC units
Endoscopies: >50
Cardiac Stress Tests: 35
Hemodialysis: 30

During the most intense period of *Comfort* MTF operations, the medical specialty areas of critical care nursing, anesthesiology, intensive care medicine, and orthopedics were most affected by the volume and acuity of the casualties admitted over a short time interval. Cross-leveling personnel from the USNS *Mercy* CUIC at NMC San Diego rectified pre-deployment critical specialty shortfalls in these areas. To meet surge requirements, the NAVCENT surgeon chose to "cross deck" additional staff from the CRTS and Bahrain surgical teams.

To put *Comfort*'s participation in OIF into perspective, the hospital ship's workload was comparable to that of the two Vietnam-era hospital ships during an especially intense period of the Vietnam War. *Comfort*'s OIF workload was similar to the median of inpatient admission statistics and the upper percentiles of major surgery statistics of the Vietnam-era hospital ships.

In the six weeks that *Comfort* was on station in the NAG, the crew again demonstrated that the MTF is a very capable and flexible medical platform. In its primary mission of combat casualty care, the hospital ship's role was to (1) care for those casualties whose injuries were so complex or who were so unstable that they were deemed too risky to make a long medical evacuation flight to the Landstuhl, Germany, army hospital, and (2) care for those casualties whose injuries were minimal and might be able to return to duty with their unit after a limited rehabilitation period. The secondary mission of humanitarian assistance was also performed by the *Comfort,* with the majority of the medical care rendered during OIF to Iraqi civilians. The mission of caring for enemy prisoners of war (EPWs) and displaced civilians was a first for *Comfort.* This was a learning experience, especially in the areas of force protection and foreign language communication barriers.

Fleet Hospitals

Navy FHs are prepositioned forward around the globe, both on shore and on maritime prepositioning force (MPF) ships. FH personnel are assigned to CONUS MTF CUICs. For OIF, Fleet Hospitals Bremerton, Pensacola, and Portsmouth personnel were deployed. The FH personnel packages are maintained according to a three-tiered readiness rotation plan, which allows for immediate activation and deployment of two Tier I FH crews. Tier I crews have recently completed an Operational Readiness Evaluation and have a greater than 90 percent readiness rating. For OIF the capability requirement was for EMF-sized fleet hospital units, so FH commanding officers exercised their ability to create a task-organized personnel package based on the mission and expected casualties estimates. The CUIC concept worked extremely well, and FH crews demonstrated excellent unit cohesion, training competency, and operational integrity.

Of the three FHs activated in support of OIF, two were requested by the combatant commander for direct support of combat operations in Iraq, and the third unit was requested as a theater evacuation hospital in Rota, Spain. FHs are currently packaged to deploy as a 116-bed expeditionary medical facility (EMF) or as a 500-bed FH. FHs 3 and 15 were off-loaded in Kuwait from Marine Corps MPF ships to support combat operations. Both of these FHs were configured to deploy as 116-bed EMFs or 500-bed FHs. The FH 3 EMF was deployed on 24 March 2003 into Iraq with a task-organized crew of 255 personnel as the first-ever fleet hospital unit to operate directly in a war zone. FH 3 treated 1,000 patients and performed 280 surgeries. FH 15's task-organized crew of 255 remained at the ready in Kuwait for the duration of the conflict. FH 8 was transported from its prepositioned site in Europe to Rota, and was fully capable as an EMF on 22 February 2003. During ground combat operations additional FH resources were deployed to Rota and facility capability was expanded to 250 beds. FH 8's task-organized crew of 250 personnel treated 1,380 inpatients and performed 262 surgeries. The unit was downsized to 100 beds after the conclusion of combat operations and remained operational until July 2003.

USMC Combat Medical Support—Naval Medicine provides health care to Marines both in peace and at war. Approximately 75,000 Marines deployed to support OIF operations representing a significant combat casualty and DNBI population at risk. The Marine Corps contained the largest concentration of organic Navy medical personnel in Iraq (2,048). The Marine Corps also received the largest Navy medical augmentation of 970 active duty personnel from CONUS MTFs and 343 medical reserves, including a significant requirement for Fleet Marine Force 8,404 hospital corpsmen. A total of four active duty and two reserve surgical companies along with ten shock trauma platoons (STPs) were deployed to support USMC operations during OIF. The care provided to wounded Marines by Navy medical personnel supporting I Marine Expeditionary Force operations during OIF led to the lowest died of wounds (DOW) rate (1.22 percent) for a major conflict in USMC history.

The health services battalion reorganized and created new capability sets to meet operational needs when variations occurred to the original medical support plan, such as shortfalls in communications, utilities gear, and limited in-country organic lift capability. By creating three reinforced surgical companies and utilizing deployed medical personnel to man the forward resuscitative surgery system (FRSS), equipment shortfalls were overcome while creating greater flexibility and capability to support maneuver warfare. The FRSS is a new capability that performed well in Iraqi Freedom. The FRSS is staffed with a team of two general surgeons, one anesthesiologist, one critical care nurse, and four corpsmen. The FRSS can accommodate eighteen casualties in forty-eight hours without resupply from the rear.

The FRSS teams served in two different capacities during OIF. One function was to serve as the initial surgical capability of a surgical company. The other was to serve as a forward surgical capability in close support of 1st Marine Division's regimental combat teams (RCTs). Because of the speed and distance covered by the Marine combat troops, the battlefield hospital corpsmen, the STPs, and the FRSS "Devil Docs" provided "golden hour" life-sustaining care far forward. The six FRSS teams treated ninety-six casualties and performed 153 operative procedures during combat operations. Because of its small size, limited resources, and mobility requirement, the FRSS has limited ability to care for postoperative patients.

A significant number of patients treated required extensive resources, for example mechanical ventilation, intravenous medications, fluid resuscitation, and blood transfusions to stabilize blood pressure. These critical medical requirements created a need for rapid medevac after stabilization surgery. Sixteen of the ninety-six casualties treated at an FRSS required en route care. Acutely ill patients requiring the aforementioned interventions were moved with the equipment, medication, and supplies needed for continuing treatment from the FRSS/STP to medical facilities in the rear by en route care nurses. The longest of these moves entailed use of rotary wing, fixed wing, and ground transport from areas outside Baghdad to the Army 47th Combat Support Hospital in Kuwait City, a distance of more than 350 miles. Usual transport was to the nearest higher level of care and averaged just less than one hour. Transport was usually by U.S. Army UH-60 Blackhawk or USMC CH-46 or CH-53 lift of opportunity.

The three surgical companies provided forward surgery and a holding capability for casualties requiring movement to higher levels of care. Established at four different general logistical staging area locations in Kuwait and Iraq, the surgical companies leapfrogged their capabilities forward in support of the rapidly moving RCTs. The surgical companies treated more than 700 patients, including 81 Iraqi civilians and 227 EPWs, and they performed 180 operative procedures.

Reserve Backfill

Traditional wartime planning factors call for an 80 percent backfill at CONUS MTFs of deployed Navy medical personnel. Reserve medical personnel backfill provides MTFs with the capability to support care of returning casualties, provide beneficiary continuity of care, and preserve graduate medical education programs. A total of 1,619 reserves mobilized to Navy MTFs for OIF backfill support roles. This represented only 42 percent backfill of the deployed active duty MTF personnel. Because casualty levels and the duration of full combat operations were less than expected, the reduced backfill was sufficient. MTFs increased operating hours, cancelled staff leave periods, and curtailed staff liberty to meet the casualty care and continuity of care mission requirements. Essentially, personnel remaining at or mobilized to CONUS MTFs "deployed at home" worked at a pace that probably would have been unsustainable over a long period. Despite the availability of civilian TRICARE network care services, a longer duration conflict would very likely have required higher backfill levels to sustain casualty care and continued operations. (Note: TRICARE is the Department of Defense health care program for active duty and retired members of the uniformed services, their families, and survivors.)

Quick Look Assessment of Naval Medicine's Wartime Performance

Agile, responsive, decisive, and sustained medical capabilities on target are what naval medicine provided during OIF. While the lessons learned are still being gathered and analyzed, some key preliminary observations are:

The *Comfort* provided early and sustained capability, but
    Too big, too slow to meet future war-fighting requirements

The EMF in a combat zone worked well, but
    Need smaller, more-mobile capability and advanced shelter technologies
    Logistics support far forward is problematic
    Digital radiography should replace conventional radiography at all care levels

Fleet hospitals employed in a communication zone worked well
    Aeromedical evacuation from theater of operation worked as designed when the FH was integrated with USAF personnel
    Concept of employment proved flexible, sustainable, and responsive to changing casualty needs
    116-bed EMF and further expansion to 250-bed FH worked well as an aeromedical Level III evacuation hospital

Forward resuscitative surgery system worked well
    Highly successful far forward capability
    Anecdotally, no one exceeded the "golden hour"
    Logistics support far forward is problematic

> Ambulance support of rapid-maneuver combat units is a challenge

Force health protection successes
> Immunizations and chem/bio identification capability
> Anecdotally, battle casualties exceeded DNBI

Displaced person and EPW medical care
> Trauma more severe than most coalition force casualties

En route care support and capabilities
> Not ideal in practice—needs some improvement and further analysis

Component unit identification code and tiered readiness
> Worked as planned in all cases
> Enabled rapid personnel identification and response
> Greater emphasis required on individual medical readiness
> More routine training on expeditionary medicine competencies required

Phased platform staffing
> Caused less disruption to CONUS MTF operations and enabled task organization of forces

Limited reserve backfill at MTFs (less than 50 percent).
> Enabled continued operations
> Level of effort sustainability very questionable over longer period

Total health care support readiness requirement model
> Responsive to war-fighter OPLAN requirements
> We had the right people to do all missions
> Critical wartime specialty manning depth challenges exist

The Way Ahead

Just as Operation Desert Storm's lessons-learned analysis provided the impetus for the development of the Total Health Care Support Readiness Requirement model, the CONUS Healthcare Readiness Infrastructure Sizing model, and CUICs, so too will Operation Iraqi Freedom yield important lessons learned and provide an impetus for future transformation. While we clearly delivered "medical capabilities on target" in support of OIF, caution must be taken not to draw quick conclusions about the readiness structure and size of naval medicine. The actual air/ground offensive combat operations ended swiftly with limited casualties. Still, naval medicine demonstrated a high level of competency in the four core qualities of naval forces: decisiveness, sustainability, responsiveness, and agility.

The author wishes to gratefully recognize the research and other contributions of Comdr. James Mitchell, MSC, USN; HMCS Dianne Proctor, USN; Mr. James Anderson; Capt. Patrick Kelly, MSC, USN; Capt. Charles Blankenship; and Capt. Harold Bohman, MSC, USN.

Overview of Recent Naval Strategy

6

From almost the immediate end of World War II, U.S. naval strategy has been shaped by the demands of the Cold War. With the end of the Cold War, that naval strategy has necessarily been in transition. While the orderly process of this change has been buffeted by numerous real-world events (Operation Desert Storm, Haiti, Somalia, Kosovo, North Korean ballistic missile tests, Chinese intercept of U.S. surveillance aircraft, Operation Enduring Freedom, Operation Noble Eagle, Operation Iraqi Freedom, and Liberia, to name a few), naval leadership has produced a number of white papers outlining changing strategic thought and direction.

To try to give the reader an overview of post–Cold War developments in naval strategy, the following are summaries of (and World Wide Web link information for) a series of Navy white papers outlining changes in U.S. naval strategy during the 1990s. The next chapter provides an overview of current U.S. naval strategy. Included here:

" . . . From the Sea" (1992)
"Forward . . . From the Sea" (1994)
"Operational Maneuver . . . From the Sea" (1996)
"Forward . . . From the Sea: How the Navy Operates"(1997)

" . . . From the Sea" (1992)

The world has changed dramatically in the last two years, and America's national security policy has also changed. As a result, the priorities of the Navy and Marine Corps have shifted, leading to this broad assessment of the future direction of our maritime forces.

The fundamental shift in national security policy was first articulated by the president at the Aspen Institute on 2 August 1990. The new policy is reflected in the president's national security strategy and the "base force" concept developed by the secretary of defense and the chairman of the Joint Chiefs of Staff.

This national security strategy has profound implications for the Navy and Marine Corps. Our strategy has shifted from a focus on a global threat to a focus on regional challenges and opportunities. While the prospect of global war has receded, we are entering a period of enormous uncertainty in regions critical to our national interests. Our forces can help to shape the future in ways favorable to our interests by underpinning our alliances, precluding threats, and helping to preserve the strategic position we won with the end of the Cold War.

Our naval forces will be full participants in the principal elements of this strategy—strategic deterrence and defense, forward presence, crisis response, and reconstitution.

With a far greater emphasis on joint and combined operations, our Navy and Marine Corps will provide unique capabilities of indispensable value in meeting our future security challenges. American naval forces provide powerful yet unobtrusive presence, strategic deterrence, control of the seas, and extended and continuous on-scene crisis response; project precise power from the sea; and provide sealift if larger-scale war-fighting scenarios emerge. These maritime capabilities are particularly well tailored for the forward presence and crisis response missions articulated in the president's national security strategy.

Our ability to command the seas in areas where we anticipate future operations allows us to resize our naval forces and to concentrate more on capabilities required in the complex operating environment of the littoral areas, or coastlines, of the earth. With the demise of the Soviet Union, the free nations of the world claim preeminent control of the seas and ensure freedom of commercial maritime passage. As a result, our national maritime policies can afford to de-emphasize efforts in some naval warfare areas. But the challenge is much more complex than simply reducing our present naval forces. We must structure a fundamentally different naval force to respond to strategic demands, and that new force must be sufficiently flexible and powerful to satisfy enduring national security requirements.

The new direction of the Navy and Marine Corps team, both active and reserve, is to provide the nation:

Naval Expeditionary Forces—shaped for joint operations
Operating Forward from the Sea—tailored for national needs

This strategic direction, derived from the national security strategy, represents a fundamental shift away from open-ocean war fighting on the sea toward joint operations conducted from the sea. The Navy and Marine Corps will now respond to crises and can provide the initial "enabling" capability for joint operations in conflict—as well as continued participation in any sustained effort. We will be part of a sea-air-land team trained to respond immediately to the unified commanders as they execute national policy.

In addition to our new direction, the Navy has a continuing obligation to maintain a robust strategic deterrent by sending nuclear ballistic submarines to sea. As long as the United States maintains a policy of nuclear deterrence, our highly survivable nuclear powered ballistic missile submarines will remain critical to national security. We also need to turn our attention and explore potential naval contributions to other forms of conventional strategic defense. In particular, we are carefully examining the naval capabilities that could contribute to theater missile defenses.

Beyond the shift in emphasis for the naval forces, there are some traditional naval missions for which we must redouble our efforts to improve our capability. Of particular importance, sealift is an enduring mission for the Navy. Our nation must remain capable of delivering heavy equipment and resupplying major ground and air combat power forward in crisis. Sealift is the key to force sustaining joint operations, and we are committed to a strong national sealift capability.

The complete text can be found at http://www.chinfo.navy. mil/navpalib/policy/fromsea/fromsea.txt

"Forward . . . From the Sea" (1994)

With the publication of " . . . From the Sea" in September 1992, the Navy and Marine Corps announced a landmark shift in operational focus and a reordering of coordinated priorities of the naval service. This fundamental shift was a direct result of the changing strategic landscape—away from having to deal with a global maritime threat and toward projecting power and influence across the seas in response to regional challenges.

In the two years since . . . From the Sea became our strategic concept, the administration has provided expanded guidance on the role of the military in national defense. A major review of strategy and force requirements resulted in a shift in the Department of Defense's focus to new dangers—chief among which is aggression by regional powers—and the necessity for our military forces to be able to rapidly project decisive military power to protect vital U.S. interests and defend friends and allies. In defining our national strategy for responding to these new dangers, the review emphasized the importance of maintaining forward-deployed naval forces and recognized the impact of peacetime operational tempo on the size of Navy and Marine Corps force structure. In addition to recognizing the unique contributions of the Navy and Marine Corps in the areas of power projection and forward presence, it restated the need for the Navy to support the national strategic objectives through our enduring contributions in strategic deterrence, sea control and maritime supremacy, and strategic sealift.

"Forward . . . From the Sea" addresses these naval contributions to our national security. Most fundamentally, our naval forces are designed to fight and win wars. Our most recent experiences, however, underscore the premise that the most important role of naval forces in situations short of war is to be engaged in forward areas, with the objectives of preventing conflicts and controlling crises.

Naval forces thus are the foundation of peacetime forward presence operations and overseas response to crisis. They contribute heavily during the transitions from crisis to conflict and to ensuring compliance with terms of peace. At the same time, the unique capabilities inherent in naval expeditionary forces have never been in higher demand from U.S. theater commanders—the regional commanders in chief—as evidenced by operations in Somalia, Haiti, Cuba, and Bosnia, as well as our continuing contribution to the enforcement of United Nations sanctions against Iraq.

The complete text can be found at http://www.chinfo.Navy.mil/navpalib/policy/fromsea/forward.txt

"Operational Maneuver . . . From the Sea" (1996)

In the white papers " . . . From the Sea" and "Forward . . . From the Sea," the secretary of the navy, with the chief of naval operations and commandant of the Marine Corps, began the development of a new approach to naval operations. This approach places unprecedented emphasis on littoral areas, requires more intimate cooperation between forces afloat and forces ashore, introduces the concept of the naval expeditionary force, and provides the foundation for operational maneuver from the sea.

Like its predecessor, the approach to amphibious warfare developed at Quantico during the 1930s, operational maneuver from the sea is a response to both danger and opportunity. The danger, summarized by the phrase "chaos in the littorals," consists of a world characterized by the clash of the myriad forces of national aspiration, religious intolerance, and ethnic hatred. The opportunity comes from significant enhancements in information management, battlefield mobility, and the lethality of conventional weapons.

These two changes to the operational environment, a new series of threats and enhanced tactical capabilities, are significant ones. While they change neither the nature of war nor our fundamental doctrine of maneuver warfare, "chaos in the littorals" and the military applications of new technologies will have a profound effect on where we fight, who we fight, and how we fight. This, in turn, will require considerable alterations in the education of leaders, the organization and equipment of units, and the selection and training of Marines.

The details of these alterations are, as yet, unknown. Refocusing the Marine Corps to meet the needs of the next century will, like all successful military innovation, involve a great deal of debate and experimentation. Many ideas will be put forward, discussed, and put to the test in war games, field trials, exercises, and actual operations. And, if history is any guide, the conclusions we draw from this process may well bear little resemblance to the assumptions with which we started.

The purpose of this concept paper is to begin this process of proposal, debate, and experimentation. Building on the foundation laid by " . . . From the Sea" and "Forward . . . From the Sea," it provides our vision of what operational maneuver from the sea is and what naval forces of the near future should be able to do. In doing this it provides a framework for the actions of many people, Marines, Sailors, civilian employees, and contractors whose work will turn the concept of operational maneuver from the sea into the reality of forces capable of winning decisive victories in littoral areas.

The complete text can be found at http://192.156.75.102/omfts.htm

"Forward . . . From the Sea:
How the Navy Operates" (1997)

The Navy's unique contributions to national security stem from the advantages of operating on, under, above, and from the sea. This is the message of "Forward . . . From the Sea." The primary purpose of forward-deployed naval forces is to project American power from the sea to influence events ashore in the littoral regions of the world across the operational spectrum of peace, crisis, and war. That is what we do. This paper describes how we do it today, and how we will do it in the future.

The roles of America's armed forces are defined by the three components of the national military strategy: peacetime engagement, deterrence and conflict prevention, and fight and win. Although national policy changes as the strategic landscape evolves, there will be continued emphasis on using the armed forces across this spectrum. Operations in peacetime and crisis to maintain regional economic and political stability are traditional roles of the Navy–Marine Corps team. These roles are rooted in our fundamental ability to maneuver independently of political constraints and fight and win. A key operational advantage of forward-deployed naval forces is that we provide on-scene capabilities for simultaneously executing all three components of the national military strategy and do so without infringing on any nation's sovereignty. This advantage exists because we operate in international waters. Our hallmark is forward-deployed forces with the highest possible readiness and capability to transition instantly from peace to crisis to conflict. This flexibility positions us to fight and win early, or to contain conflict. More importantly, our presence may prevent conflict altogether. By any standard or measure, peace is cheaper than war.

Our forces are optimized for this forward role in national strategy. As we enter the twenty-first century, we will continue to develop and adopt innovative concepts and technologies to remain the force on the cutting edge of our nation's defense.

How the Navy Operates

"Forward . . . From the Sea" provides the basis for a simple, yet powerful operational concept of how we will operate to carry out expeditionary operations. We conduct forward naval operations both to ensure unimpeded use of the seas and to project American influence and power into the littoral areas of the world. Expeditionary operations achieve U.S. objectives across the spectrum of the national military strategy. They are a potent and cost-effective alternative to power projection from the continental United States and are ideally suited for the many contingencies that can be deterred or quickly handled by forward-deployed forces. Expeditionary operations complement, enable, and dramatically enhance the effectiveness of continental power-projection forces when a larger military response is needed.

Our attention and efforts will continue to be focused on operating in and from the littorals. The landward side of the littoral can be supported and defended directly from the sea. It encompasses areas of strategic importance to the United States. Seventy-five percent of the earth's population and a similar proportion of national capitals and major commercial centers lie in the littorals. These are the places where American influence and power have the greatest impact and are needed most often. For forward-deployed naval forces, the littorals are a starting point as well as a destination. Tactically, the distance we reach inland from the sea depends on terrain and weather, the contributions of joint and coalition forces, the potential adversary's capabilities, and the nature of our mission. The mission may require us to exercise our considerable reach and operate far inland.

We will deploy carrier battle groups and amphibious ready groups with embarked Marines to provide naval expeditionary forces for the combatant commanders. When required, we deploy separate units—such as for maritime interception force operations—but each remains capable of being integrated into a larger naval expeditionary force.

We train carrier battle groups and amphibious ready groups together to ensure immediate readiness for a wide range of contingencies. Once overseas we disperse the force and maintain a dynamic presence posture. Our forces are constantly in motion to make their capabilities visible throughout the theater while carrying out numerous simultaneous missions in support of U.S. interests.

We can operate individual units—such as submarines—independently or completely integral to the force. We link dispersed units as an integrated force with command and control networks. When necessary for a specific crisis-response operation, we rapidly assemble elements of the force into a mission-tailored task group, such as a surface battle group.

We rapidly converge from our forward deployment hubs to the scene of a potential conflict to deter aggression or to project power should deterrence fail.

We take advantage of the reach of our sensors and weapons to project power over vast areas from a dispersed, networked force—concentrating combat power rather than our platforms and delivering firepower far inland when required by the mission.

We are on-scene and ready for peacetime engagement, deterrence and conflict prevention, and fighting and winning.

The complete text can be found at http://www.chinfo.Navy.mil/navpalib/policy/fromsea/ffseanoc.html

Current Naval Vision: Sea Power 21 7

The text in this chapter is condensed from a series of articles published in the U.S. Naval Institute's *Proceedings* magazine. This series of articles detailed the current naval vision expressed by Adm. Vern Clark, chief of naval operations (CNO), and senior members of the Navy staff. These articles include:

Bucchi, Mike, and Mike Mullen. "Sea Shield: Projecting Global Defensive Assurance" (November 2002).

Clark, Vern. "Sea Power 21: Projecting Decisive Joint Capabilities" (October 2002).

Dawson, Cutler, and John Nathman. "Sea Strike: Projecting Persistent, Responsive, and Precise Power" (December 2002).

Harms, Alfred G., Jr., Gerald L. Hoewing, and John B. Totushek. "Sea Warrior: Maximizing Human Capital" (June 2003).

Mayo, Richard W., and John Nathman. "ForceNet: Turning Information into Power" (February 2003).

Moore, Charles W., Jr., and Edward Hanlon Jr. "Sea Basing: Operational Independence for a New Century" (January 2003).

Mullen, Michael G. "Sea Enterprise: Resourcing Tomorrow's Fleet" (January 2004).

Natter, Robert J. "Sea Trial: Enabler for a Transformed Fleet" (November 2003).

Sea Power 21: Projecting Decisive Joint Capabilities

Our Vision
The twenty-first century sets the stage for tremendous increases in naval precision, reach, and connectivity, ushering in a new era of joint operational effectiveness. Innovative concepts and technologies will integrate sea, land, air, space, and cyberspace to a greater

extent than ever before. In this unified battle space, the sea will provide a vast maneuver area from which to project direct and decisive power around the globe.

Future naval operations will use revolutionary information superiority and dispersed, networked force capabilities to deliver unprecedented offensive power, defensive assurance, and operational independence to joint force commanders. We will continue the evolution of U.S. naval power from the blue-water, war-at-sea focus of the "Maritime Strategy" (1986), through the littoral emphasis of " . . . From the Sea" (1992) and "Forward . . . from the Sea" (1994), to a broadened strategy in which naval forces are fully integrated into global joint operations against regional and transnational dangers.

To realize the opportunities and navigate the challenges ahead, we must have a clear vision of how our Navy will organize, integrate, and transform. "Sea Power 21" is that vision.

Transformation for a Violent Era

Previous strategies addressed regional challenges. Today, we must think more broadly. Enhancing security in this dynamic environment requires us to expand our strategic focus to include both evolving regional challenges and transnational threats. This combination of traditional and emerging dangers means increased risk to our nation. To counter that risk, our Navy must expand its striking power, achieve information dominance, and develop transformational ways of fulfilling our enduring missions of sea control, power projection, strategic deterrence, strategic sealift, and forward presence.

Three fundamental concepts lie at the heart of the Navy's continued operational effectiveness: Sea Strike, Sea Shield, and Sea Basing. Sea Strike is the ability to project precise and persistent offensive power from the sea; Sea Shield extends defensive assurance throughout the world; and Sea Basing enhances operational independence and support for the joint force.

Sea Strike, Sea Shield, and Sea Basing will be enabled by ForceNet, an overarching effort to integrate warriors, sensors, networks, command and control, platforms, and weapons into a fully netted, combat force. We have been talking about network-centric warfare for a decade, and ForceNet will be the Navy's plan to make it an operational reality. Supported by ForceNet, Sea Strike, Sea Shield, and Sea Basing capabilities will be deployed by way of a global concept of operations that widely distributes the fire-power of the fleet, strengthens deterrence, improves crisis response, and positions us to win decisively in war.

The complete text can be found at http://www.chinfo.navy.mil/navpalib/cno/proceedings.html

Sea Shield: Projecting Global Defensive Assurance

In his October 2002 *Proceedings* article "Sea Power 21," the CNO prescribes a broadened naval strategy that will fully integrate U.S. naval forces into joint operations against regional and transnational dangers. He rededicates the Navy to a global focus that will dissuade, deter, and defeat a growing array of potential threats, including weapons of mass destruction, conventional warfare, and widely dispersed and well-funded terrorism.

Three interwoven operational concepts lie at the heart of his vision: Sea Strike, Sea Shield, and Sea Basing. Sea Strike, the projection of precise and persistent offensive power, will punish aggressors swiftly and decisively. Sea Shield will provide a layered defense to protect the homeland, sustain access to contested littorals, and project a defensive umbrella over coalition partners and joint forces ashore in distant theaters. Sea Basing of joint warfighting capabilities by way of a widely distributed and netted fleet will increase the operational independence of U.S. forces and serve as the foundation for the projection of offensive and defensive fires—making Sea Strike and Sea Shield a reality.

Sea Shield embraces emerging technologies and concepts that for the first time have the potential to extend naval defensive firepower beyond the task force. Sea Shield encompasses some things great navies always have tried to do—sea control off hostile coasts and maritime defense of the homeland, for example—and some that no navy has ever done, such as projecting defense deep inland against cruise and ballistic missiles.

The complete text is available to members of the U.S. Naval Institute at http://www.usni.org/proceedings/proceedings.html

Sea Strike: Projecting Persistent, Responsive, and Precise Power

Sea Strike is a vision of what we will become as well as the focus of our capability today. It is about far more than putting bombs on target, although the delivery of ordnance remains a critical function. At its heart, Sea Strike is a broad concept for naval power projection that leverages command, control, communications, computers, combat systems, intelligence, surveillance, and reconnaissance (C^5ISR), precision, stealth, information, and joint strike together.

The complete text is available to members of the U.S. Naval Institute at http://www.usni.org/proceedings/proceedings.html

Sea Basing: Operational Independence for a New Century

Sea Basing is the core of "Sea Power 21." It is about placing at sea—to a greater extent than ever before—capabilities critical to joint and coalition operational success: offensive and defensive firepower, maneuver forces, command and control, and logistics. By doing so, it minimizes the need to build up forces and supplies ashore, reduces their vulnerability, and enhances operational mobility. It leverages advanced sensor and communications systems, precision ordnance, and weapons reach while prepositioning joint capabilities where they are immediately employable and most decisive. It exploits the operational shift in warfare from mass to precision and information, employing the 70 percent of the earth's surface that is covered with water as a vast maneuver area in support of the joint force.

Sea Basing will be increasingly central to joint military planning because the traditional *advantages* enjoyed by afloat forces—such as independence, mobility, and security—are becoming ever more important to military affairs, while traditional *limitations* of sea-based forces—including operational reach and connectivity—have been largely overcome by new technologies and concepts of operations. These advances in sea-based capabilities could not come at a more critical time, as political and military barriers to access ashore are growing worldwide. Because of these changes, the value of Sea Basing in an increasingly interdependent world will continue to rise—providing operational freedom for joint and coalition forces, compressing deployment timelines, strengthening deterrence, and projecting dominant and decisive combat power from the sea.

In a world of hidden and fleeting enemies, Sea Basing provides the joint force commander with dispersed, netted, and sovereign platforms that are ready to respond. To accomplish this mission, the sea base is comprised of distributed forces of many types, in-

cluding carrier strike groups, expeditionary strike groups, combat
logistics force ships, maritime prepositioning force platforms, and,
in the years ahead, high-speed support vessels. Working together,
these forces mass effects rather than platforms, increasing sensor
coverage and force protection while focusing offensive and defensive firepower throughout the battle space. This increase in operational effectiveness is possible because naval capabilities are
evolving in important ways.

The complete text is available to members of the U.S. Naval
Institute at http://www.usni.org/proceedings/proceedings.html

ForceNet: Turning Information into Power

The information age has dramatically increased U.S. combat effectiveness. New communications links, computer-processing
techniques, and miniaturized electronics have given the U.S.
armed forces global connectivity, powerful sensors, and weapons
with awesome precision and lethality. By more fully integrating
these technical capabilities with twenty-first-century warriors,
ForceNet will deliver the full promise of network-centric warfare.

Swift and effective use of information will be central to the
success of "Sea Power 21." Sea Strike will rely on rich situational
awareness provided by persistent intelligence, surveillance, and
reconnaissance to sense hostile capabilities and trigger rapid and
precise attacks. Sea Shield will use integrated information from
joint military, interagency, and coalition sources to identify and
neutralize threats far from our shores, locate and destroy anti-
access challenges in littoral waters, and intercept missiles deep
over land. Sea Basing will draw on comprehensive data to sustain
critical functions afloat, such as joint command and logistics, ensuring operational effectiveness and timely support.

Near-instantaneous collection, analysis, and dissemination of
information coupled to advanced computer-driven decision aids
will unify the battle space of the twenty-first century, turning the
seas into joint maneuver areas. This vital asymmetric advantage of
information superiority will increase responsiveness and surviv-
ability by allowing our forces to disperse while focusing offensive
and defensive firepower over tremendous distances. ForceNet will
provide the information that enables knowledge-based operations,
delivering greater power, protection, and operational independence than ever before possible to joint force commanders.

The complete text is available to members of the U.S. Naval Institute at http://www.usni.org/proceedings/proceedings.html

Sea Warrior: Maximizing Human Capital

The Navy's human resource system produces trained Sailors to man the fleet. "Sea Power 21" demands much more. Our striking groups deployed over the past two years have been increasingly better manned as a result of a host of personnel and manpower initiatives, but we still have much to do if we are to optimize our Navy's personnel readiness. We must find a way to get each individual—consistently, systematically, and comprehensively—into the job of maximum potential.

Shaped by the conscription demands of World War II, then the Cold War, and then more than a decade of draw down, our processes and systems understandably were not designed with the individual at the center. So it should not surprise us, in today's all-volunteer environment, that we see some misalignments and inefficiencies. Neither should it surprise us that transformation is within our grasp.

This is the goal of Sea Warrior: to integrate the Navy's manpower, personnel, and training organizations—active and reserve—into a single, efficient, information-rich human resource management system. Its focus is on growing individuals from the moment they walk into a recruiting office through their assignments as master chiefs or flag officers, using a career continuum of training and education that gives them the tools they need to operate in an increasingly demanding and dynamic environment. Through Sea Warrior, we will identify Sailors' precise capabilities and match them to well-articulated job requirements that far exceed the simplistic criteria used today. In addition, we will implement different types of incentives and flexible rotation dates and move the Navy toward a job-based compensation system.

From an acquisition perspective, this means designing our platforms and systems with war-fighter performance as a key parameter. For commands, it means a market-based, near-real-time process that responds rapidly and efficiently to the manpower, personnel, and training demands of an expeditionary service.

The result is not simply trained Sailors to the fleet, but a quantum leap in fleet effectiveness through efficient development and assignment of optimally trained, motivated manpower.

The complete text is available to members of the U.S. Naval Institute at http://www.usni.org/proceedings/proceedings.html

Sea Trial: Enabler for a Transformed Fleet

Lieutenant Paul Jones has just launched two unmanned underwater vehicles (UUVs) from the littoral combat ship *Arrowhead*. Working with the USS *Virginia* (SSN-774) below the surface and an overhead swarm of unmanned aerial vehicles (UAVs) launched by the *Arrowhead*'s sister ships, the lieutenant is part of a sustained, littoral reconnaissance effort. In minutes, he receives confirmation that the UUVs are up and sweet in the net. His commanding officer is using all of his ship's nearly 50-knot speed to reposition outside the range of an enemy coastal defense cruise missile battery spotted by one of the UAVs. Jones thinks to himself that the battery will be a hellish place to be once hypersonic projectiles begin raining down from the destroyer 100 miles to seaward. As he checks the hyperspectral imagery coming from the UAVs, Jones receives a videoconference call on his personal communicator from his commanding officer. The captain of the *Virginia* and a SEAL platoon commander are in the conference as well. They already are recommending to the joint force commander the immediate insertion of special forces ashore. This is going to be a busy day for Lieutenant Jones and the rest of the *Arrowhead*'s crew."

The technology at Lieutenant Jones's fingertips is in development now. How effective it will be in combat depends on the processes—known broadly as concepts of operations (ConOps) and doctrine—we develop to harness its potential. Simply grafting new technology to old processes will not work. To fully leverage the advantages technology brings, we must speed up our process of innovation and coevolve concepts, technologies, and doctrine.

Sea Trial will drive that coevolution.

In the Navy's strategic concept for the twenty-first century, "Sea Power 21," CNO Admiral Clark designated Commander, U.S. Fleet Forces Command (CFFC), as the executive agent for Sea Trial. The reason is simple. Because the Navy starts with the fleet, the fleet must drive innovation and experimentation. Sea Trial cannot be dictated from programming offices in Washington, D.C., nor can systems commands alone foster it. It will require the active involvement of our operators in the testing and evaluation of the technology provided by systems commands and the tactics and doctrine developed by warfare centers of excellence. That depth of integration is possible only at the fleet level—and it is only through that kind of integration that we can generate the intellectual synergy necessary for experimentation and discovery. In the end, this process is about unleashing the creative genius of our people.

As executive agent for Sea Trial, CFFC integrates the efforts of the Second and Third Fleet commanders, along with the commander of Network Warfare Command, as they sponsor concept development and experimentation to develop Sea Strike, Sea Shield, Sea Basing, and ForceNet capabilities. These commanders will reach throughout the fleet, the military, and beyond to coordinate concept and technology development in support of future warfighting effectiveness. The systems commands and program executive offices are central partners in this effort, bringing concepts to reality through innovation and the application of sound business principles. Meanwhile, our ships and aircraft will serve as sea-based laboratories, with our operators helping to answer the most pressing questions posed by this period of rapid technological change:

What new ConOps will make the most effective use of existing and emerging technologies?

What organizational changes will be necessary to achieve the most efficient execution of the new ConOps?

What new technologies must be developed to fully implement new doctrine?

Sea Trial is up and running, facilitating the transition of promising capabilities from validated concept, to experimentation and demonstration, to implementation in the fleet. This process serves both as the voice of today's war fighters and a means to look beyond current programs of record to provide the right capabilities for future generations. We will prioritize the fleet's required capabilities, share information on potential solutions, conduct sound and analytical war-gaming and experimentation, agree on a way ahead, and implement it without delay. Sea Trial also will stimulate the Navy's science and technology efforts by identifying the technologies needed to fully implement new doctrine.

The complete text is available to members of the U.S. Naval Institute at http://www.usni.org/proceedings/proceedings.html

Part Two

The Navy Today

Department of the Navy Organization

The mission of the U.S. Navy is to maintain, train, and equip combat-ready naval forces capable of winning wars, deterring aggression, and maintaining freedom of the seas. The following sections provide an overview of how the Department of the Navy is organized to accomplish that mission.

Overview of Navy Organization

The following chart presents an overview of the organization of the Department of the Navy. The U.S. Navy was founded on 13 October 1775, and the Department of the Navy was established on 30 April 1798. The Department of the Navy has three principal components: The Navy Department, consisting of executive offices mostly in Washington, D.C.; the operating forces, including the Marine Corps, the reserve components, and, in time of war, the U.S. Coast Guard (in peace, a component of the Department of Homeland Security); and the shore establishment.

Secretary of the Navy

The secretary of the navy (SECNAV) is responsible for, and has the authority under Title 10 of the United States Code to conduct, all the affairs of the Department of the Navy, including recruiting, organizing, supplying, equipping, training, mobilizing, and demobilizing. The secretary also oversees the construction, outfitting, and repair of naval ships, equipment, and facilities. SECNAV is responsible for the formulation and implementation of policies and programs that are consistent with the national security policies and objectives established by the president and the secretary of defense. The Department of the Navy consists of two uniformed services: the United States Navy and the United States Marine Corps.

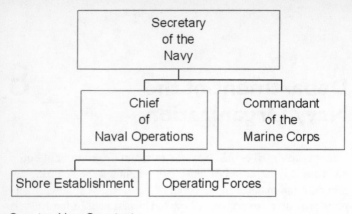

Overview Navy Organization

Office of the Chief of Naval Operations

The chief of naval operations (CNO) is the senior military officer in the Navy. The CNO is a four-star admiral and is responsible to the secretary of the navy for the command, utilization of resources, and operating efficiency of the operating forces of the Navy and of the Navy shore activities assigned by the secretary.

A member of the Joint Chiefs of Staff, the CNO is the principal naval adviser to the president and to the secretary of the navy on the conduct of war, and is the principal adviser and naval executive to the SECNAV on the conduct of naval activities of the Department of the Navy. Assistants are the Vice CNO (VCNO), the Deputy Chiefs of Naval Operations (DCNOs), and a number of other ranking officers. These officers and their staffs are collectively known as the Office of the Chief of Naval Operations (Op-Nav).

The Shore Establishment

The shore establishment provides support to the operating forces (known as "the fleet") in the form of facilities for the repair of machinery and electronics; communications centers; training areas and simulators; ship and aircraft repair; intelligence and meteorological support; storage areas for repair parts, fuel, and munitions; medical and dental facilities; and air bases.

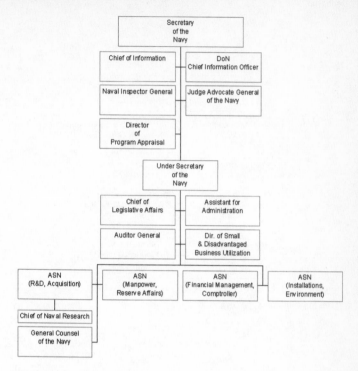

Office of the Secretary of the Navy

The operating forces commanders and fleet commanders have a dual chain of command. Administratively, they report to the CNO and provide, train, and equip naval forces. Operationally, they provide naval forces and report to the appropriate Unified Combatant Commanders. The fleet forces commander—who has additional duty as Commander, U.S. Atlantic Fleet—controls LANTFLT and Pacific Fleet (PACFLT) assets for inter-deployment training cycle purposes. As units of the Navy enter the area of responsibility for a particular Navy area commander, they are operationally assigned to the appropriate numbered fleet. All Navy units also have an administrative chain of command, with the various ships reporting to the appropriate type commander.

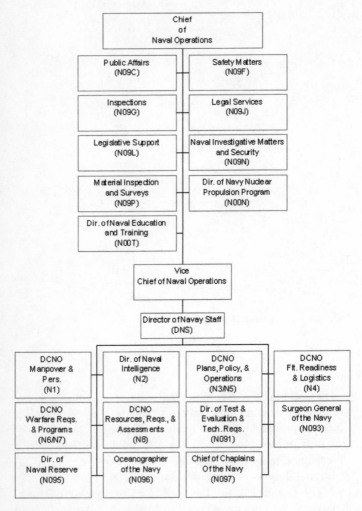

Office of the Chief of Naval Operations

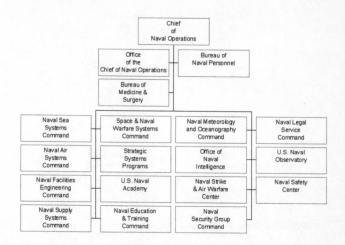

The Navy Shore Establishment

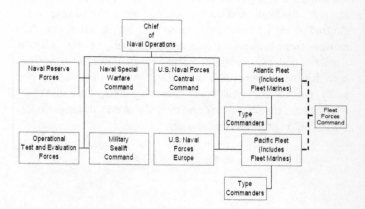

The Navy Operating Forces

The Type Commands

The Type Commands

All ships are organized into categories by type. Aircraft carriers, aircraft squadrons, and air stations are under the administrative control of the appropriate Commander Naval Air Force. Submarines come under the Commander Submarine Force. All other ships fall under Commander Naval Surface Force. Also, you will note that the Atlantic and Pacific Fleets mirror one another. Normally, the type command controls the ship during her primary and intermediate training cycles and then she moves under the operational control of a fleet commander.

Secretaries of the Navy 9

The secretary of the navy (SECNAV) is responsible for and has the authority under Title 10 of the U.S. Code of Federal Regulations to conduct all the affairs of the Department of the Navy, including recruiting, organizing, supplying, equipping, training, mobilizing, and demobilizing. The secretary also oversees the construction, outfitting, and repair of naval ships, equipment, and facilities. SECNAV is responsible for the formulation and implementation of policies and programs that are consistent with the national security policies and objectives established by the president and the secretary of defense. The Department of the Navy consists of two uniformed services: the United States Navy and the United States Marine Corps.

Name	Term of Office
Benjamin Stoddert	18 June 1798 to 31 March 1801
Robert Smith	27 July 1801 to 7 March 1809
Paul Hamilton	15 May 1809 to 31 December 1812
William Jones	19 January 1813 to 12 January 1814
Benjamin W. Crowninshield	16 January 1815 to 30 September 1818
Smith Thompson	1 January 1819 to 31 August 1823
Samuel Southard	16 September 1823 to 3 March 1829
John Branch	9 March 1829 to 12 May 1831
Levi Woodbury	23 May 1831 to 30 June 1834
Mahlon Dickerson	1 July 1834 to 30 June 1838
James K. Paulding	1 July 1838 to 3 March 1841
George E. Badger	6 March 1841 to 11 September 1841
Abel P. Upshur	11 October 1841 to 23 July 1843
David Henshaw	24 July 1843 to 18 February 1844
Thomas W. Gilmer	19 February 1844 to 28 February 1844
John Y. Mason	26 March 1844 to 10 March 1845
George Bancroft	11 March 1845 to 9 September 1846
John Y. Mason	10 September 1846 to 7 March 1849
William B. Preston	8 March 1849 to 22 July 1850
William A. Graham	2 August 1850 to 25 July 1852

John P. Kennedy	26 July 1852 to 7 March 1853
James C. Dobbin	8 March 1853 to 6 March 1857
Isaac Toucey	7 March 1857 to 6 March 1861
Gideon Welles	7 March 1861 to 3 March 1869
Adolph E. Borie	9 March 1869 to 25 June 1869
George M. Robeson	26 June 1869 to 12 March 1877
Richard W. Thompson	13 March 1877 to 20 December 1880
Nathan Goff Jr.	7 January 1881 to 6 March 1881
William H. Hunt	7 March 1881 to 16 April 1882
William E. Chandler	16 April 1882 to 6 March 1885
William C. Whitney	7 March 1885 to 5 March 1889
Benjamin F. Tracy	6 March 1889 to 6 March 1893
Hilary A. Herbert	7 March 1893 to 6 March 1897
John D. Long	6 March 1897 to 30 April 1902
William H. Moody	1 May 1902 to 30 June 1904
Paul Morton	1 July 1904 to 30 June 1905
Charles J. Bonaparte	1 July 1905 to 16 December 1906
Victor H. Metcalf	17 December 1906 to 30 November 1908
Truman H. Newberry	1 December 1908 to 5 March 1909
George von L. Meyer	6 March 1909 to 4 March 1913
Josephus Daniels	5 March 1913 to 5 March 1921
Edwin Denby	6 March 1921 to 10 March 1924
Curtis D. Wilbur	19 March 1924 to 4 March 1929
Charles F. Adams	5 March 1929 to 4 March 1933
Claude A. Swanson	4 March 1933 to 7 July 1939
Charles Edison	2 January 1940 to 24 June 1940
Frank Knox	11 July 1940 to 28 April 1944
James Forrestal	19 May 1944 to 17 September 1947
John L. Sullivan	18 September 1947 to 24 May 1949
Francis P. Matthews	25 May 1949 to 31 July 1951
Dan A. Kimball	31 July 1951 to 20 January 1953
Robert B. Anderson	4 February 1953 to 3 May 1954
Charles S. Thomas	3 May 1954 to 1 April 1957
Thomas S. Gates	1 April 1957 to 8 June 1959
William B. Franke	8 June 1959 to 19 January 1961
John B. Connally Jr.	25 January 1961 to 20 December 1961
Fred Korth	4 January 1962 to 1 November 1963
Paul B. Fay (acting)	2 November 1963 to 28 November 1963
Paul H. Nitze	29 November 1963 to 30 June 1967
Charles F. Baird (acting)	1 July 1967 to 31 August 1967
Paul R. Ignatius	1 September 1967 to 24 January 1969
John H. Chafee	31 January 1969 to 4 May 1972

John H. Warner	4 May 1972 to 8 April 1974
J. William Middendorf	8 April 1974 to 20 January 1977
W. Graham Claytor Jr.	14 February 1977 to 24 August 1979
Edward Hidalgo	24 October 1979 to 20 January 1981
John Lehman	5 February 1981 to 10 April 1987
James H. Webb	1 May 1987 to 23 February 1988
William L. Ball	28 March 1988 to 15 May 1989
Henry L. Garrett III	15 May 1989 to 26 June 1992
Sean O'Keefe (acting)	7 July 1992 to 21 July 1993
John H. Dalton	22 July 1993 to 16 November 1998
Richard Danzig	16 November 1998 to 20 January 2001
Robert B. Pirie Jr. (acting)	20 January 2001 to 24 May 2001
Gordon R. England	24 May 2001 to 24 January 2003
Susan Morissey Livington (acting)	24 January 2003 to 7 February 2003
Hanford T. Johnson (acting)	7 February 2003 to 1 October 2003
Gordon R. England*	1 October 2003 to present

*As this book went to press, Secretary England has been nominated to be the new Undersecretary of Defense.

Chiefs of Naval Operations

10

The chief of naval operations (CNO) is the senior military officer of the Department of the Navy. The CNO is a four-star admiral and is responsible to the secretary of the navy (SECNAV) for the command, utilization of resources, and operating efficiency of the operating forces of the Navy and of the Navy shore activities assigned by the secretary. A member of the Joint Chiefs of Staff, the CNO is the principal naval adviser to the president and to the SECNAV on the conduct of war, and is the principal adviser and naval executive to the secretary on the conduct of activities of the Department of the Navy. Assistants are the vice chief of naval operations (VCNO), the deputy chiefs of naval operations (DCNOs), the assistant chiefs of naval operations (ACNOs), and a number of other ranking officers. These officers and their staffs are collectively known as the office of the chief of naval operations (OpNav).

Name	Term of Office
William Shepherd Benson	11 May 1915 to 25 September 1919
Robert Edward Coontz	1 November 1919 to 21 July 1923
Edward Walter Eberle	21 July 1923 to 14 November 1927
Charles Frederick Hughes	14 November 1927 to 17 September 1930
William Veazie Pratt	17 September 1930 to 30 June 1933
William Harrison Standley	1 July 1933 to 1 January 1937
William Daniel Leahy	2 January 1937 to 1 August 1939
Harold Raynsford Stark	1 August 1939 to 26 March 1942
Ernest Joseph King	26 March 1942 to 15 December 1945
Chester William Nimitz	15 December 1945 to 15 December 1947
Louis Emil Denfeld	15 December 1947 to 1 November 1949
Forrest Percival Sherman	2 November 1949 to 22 July 1951
William Morrow Fechteler	16 August 1951 to 17 August 1953

Robert Bostwick Carney	17 August 1953 to 17 August 1955
Arleigh Albert Burke	17 August 1955 to 1 August 1961
George Whalen Anderson Jr.	1 August 1961 to 1 August 1963
David Lamar McDonald	1 August 1963 to 1 August 1967
Thomas Hinman Moorer	1 August 1967 to 1 July 1970
Elmo Russell Zumwalt Jr.	1 July 1970 to 1 July 1974
James L. Holloway III	1 July 1974 to 30 June 1978
Thomas B. Hayward	1 July 1978 to 30 June 1982
James D. Watkins	1 July 1982 to 30 June 1986
Carlisle A. H. Trost	1 July 1986 to 30 June 1990
Frank B. Kelso II	1 July 1990 to 23 April 1994
Jeremy Michael Boorda	23 April 1994 to 16 May 1996
Jay L. Johnson	2 August 1996 to 21 July 2000
Vern Clark*	21 July 2000 to present

*As this book went to press, Adm. Michael Mullen had been nominated to succeed Admiral Clark as Chief of Naval Operations in the summer of 2005.

Master Chief Petty Officers of the Navy

11

The master chief petty officer of the navy (MCPON) is the senior enlisted person in the Navy. The MCPON serves as the senior enlisted leader of the Navy and as an adviser to the chief of naval operations and to the chief of naval personnel in matters dealing with enlisted personnel and their families.

The MCPON is also an adviser to the many boards dealing with enlisted personnel issues, is the enlisted representative of the Department of the Navy at special events, may be called upon to testify on enlisted personnel issues before Congress, and maintains a liaison with enlisted spouse organizations.

The MCPON can be reached at:

Master Chief Petty Officer of the Navy
2 Navy Annex, Room 1046
Washington, D.C. 20370-2000

Name	Term of Office
Delbert Black	13 January 1967 to 1 April 1971
John D. Whittet	1 April 1971 to 25 September 1975
Robert J. Walker	26 September 1975 to 28 September 1979
Thomas S. Crow	28 September 1979 to 1 October 1982
Billy Sanders	1 October 1982 to 4 October 1985
William H. Plackett	4 October 1985 to 9 September 1988
Duane R. Bushey	9 September 1988 to 28 August 1992
John Hagan	28 August 1992 to 27 March 1998
James L. Herdt	27 March 1998 to 22 April 2002
Terry D. Scott	22 April 2002 to present

Ships of the U.S. Navy 12

The U.S. Navy operates hundreds of ships. Some of these are active ships, which means they have a full complement of personnel and, unless they are temporarily undergoing heavy maintenance or repair, are fully capable of carrying out an assigned mission on short notice.

The Navy also keeps a number of vessels in reserve status, which means they are partially manned with active duty personnel. The rest of the crew is made up of reserve personnel, who man the ships periodically for training and when called upon in a national emergency.

The Navy also operates a number of vessels under what is called the Military Sealift Command (MSC). These ships usually have only a very small contingent of Navy personnel on board, and the majority of the crews are civilians. MSC ships play a support role and are not used as frontline combatants. They are considered to be "in service" rather than "in commission." Some ships, such as roll-on, roll-off vehicle cargo ships (AKRs) and transport oilers (AOTs) serve the Army and Air Force as well as the Navy.

Other MSC ships perform special-duty projects, such as ocean-bottom laying and repairing of cables used for detecting enemy submarines. Surveying ships (AGSs) and oceanographic research ships (AGORs) explore the oceans.

Of special interest is a group of various MSC ships of the Naval Fleet Auxiliary Force (NFAF). As with other MSC ships, they have civilian officers and crews. They operate under Navy orders and have a military department of Navy personnel aboard, performing visual and radio communications and otherwise assisting the ship's civilian master and crew in operations with other naval

The following material is extracted from *The Bluejacket's Manual,* Centennial Edition (Annapolis, Md.: Naval Institute Press, 2002).

units. These vessels include a variety of replenishment ships, fleet ocean tugs, and several specialized mission types.

Ship Identification

Most Navy ships have both a name and what we call a *ship's designation* to identify them. While the name is a convenient and traditional means of identification, there have been Navy ships bearing the same name throughout history, so the ship's designation—which is unique to that ship—is the only way to identify a specific naval vessel. The ship's designation tells what *type* the ship is (such as destroyer, submarine, or cruiser) and assigns a specific *hull number* to the vessel.

Ships are also grouped into *classes* to identify those with identical, or nearly identical, characteristics.

Name

The name is unique to a ship in that there can be only one Navy ship in commission at a time with a given name. But, as mentioned previously, there may have been other ships with the same name in the past—in fact, it is fairly common practice in the Navy for ships to carry the name of an earlier ship that served with honor. For example, there have been six U.S. Navy ships named *Enterprise*. (*Note:* This count does not include the starship *Enterprise* of Star Trek fame, but the creator of the hit television and movie series, Gene Roddenberry, recognized the long tradition of passing on ship names and carried it on in his futuristic vision.)

The name of a Navy ship in commission (active or reserve) is preceded by the letters "USS," which stand for "United States Ship," for example, USS *Enterprise*. Because they are considered to be "in service" rather than "in commission," names of MSC ships are preceded by the letters "USNS" (for United States Naval Ship) instead of USS. Great Britain's Royal Navy vessels carry the prefix "HMS" before their names, which stands for "Her Majesty's Ship" (or "*His* Majesty's Ship" if there is a reigning king instead of a queen). The navies of other nations are similarly identified.

Sailors have traditionally added nicknames to their seagoing homes. Among aircraft carriers, for instance, the USS *Enterprise* is known informally as the "Big E," the *Constellation* is the "Connie," and the *Dwight D. Eisenhower* is "Ike."

Designation

While a ship's name gives her some identity, the ship's designation—which consists of a combination of letters and numbers—tells you two additional things about a ship: her type and her place in the construction sequence. The USS *Theodore Roosevelt,* for instance, has the designation CVN 71. CVN is her type classification, *CV* standing for aircraft carrier and *N* meaning nuclear propulsion; 71 indicates that she is the seventy-first aircraft carrier authorized for construction. The term *hull number* actually refers strictly to the number part of the ship's designation, but you will commonly hear it used instead of "ship's designation." Ships' hull numbers are frequently painted on their bows and near the stern. Aircraft carriers have their hull numbers painted on the forward part of the flight deck and on the "island" (superstructure).

Since 1920, the Navy has used letter symbols to identify the types of ships and service craft. This is called "type classification" and is used as part of the ship's designation. Some of the more common type classifications are listed below. Keep in mind that some of these type classifications may not be currently in use, but they are listed because you may come across them historically or they may be reactivated at some later date. Those not currently in service are listed in italics.

AD	Destroyer tender
AE	Ammunition ship
AFS	Combat store ship
AGF	Miscellaneous command ship
AH	Hospital ship
AO	Oiler
AOE	Fast combat-support ship
AOR	Replenishment oiler
APL	Barracks craft (non-self-propelled)
ARS	Salvage ship
AS	Submarine tender
ASR	Submarine rescue ship
ATF	Fleet ocean tug
BB	*Battleship*
CA	*Heavy cruiser*
CG	Guided-missile cruiser
CGN	*Guided-missile cruiser (nuclear propulsion)*
CL	*Light cruiser*

CV	Multipurpose aircraft carrier
CVA	*Attack aircraft carrier*
CVN	Multipurpose aircraft carrier (nuclear propulsion)
CVS	*Antisubmarine warfare aircraft carrier*
DD	Destroyer
DDG	Guided-missile destroyer
DE	*Destroyer escort*
DL	*Destroyer leader*
DSRV	Deep-submergence rescue vehicle
FF	*Frigate*
FFG	Guided-missile frigate
IX	Unclassified miscellaneous
LCAC	Landing craft, air cushion
LCC	Amphibious command ship
LCM	Landing craft, mechanized
LCPL	Landing craft, personnel, large
LCU	Landing craft, utility
LCVP	Landing craft, vehicle, and personnel
LHA	Amphibious assault ship (general purpose)
LHD	Amphibious assault ship (multipurpose)
LPD	Amphibious transport dock
LPH	*Amphibious assault ship (helicopter)*
LSD	Dock-landing ship
LSSC	Light SEAL support craft
LST	*Tank-landing ship*
MCM	Mine-countermeasures ship
MCS	*Mine-countermeasures support ship*
MHC	Coastal minehunter
MSC	*Coastal minesweeper*
MSO	*Ocean-going minesweeper*
PBR	River patrol boat
PC	Coastal patrol craft
PCF	*Fast patrol craft ("swift boat")*
PT	*Patrol torpedo boat*
SS	*Submarine*
SSBN	Ballistic-missile submarine (nuclear propulsion)
SSN	Submarine (nuclear propulsion)
YP	Yard patrol
YTB	Large Harbor Tug
YTL	Small Harbor Tug
YTM	Medium Harbor Tug

Ships of the MSC are distinguished from other Navy ships by having a "T" before their letter designations. Below are some examples of MSC ship types.

T-AFS	Combat stores ship
T-AE	Ammunition ships
T-ATF	Fleet ocean tug
T-AH	Hospital ship
T-AGOS	Ocean surveillance ship
T-AGS	Oceanographic Survey
T-ARC	Cable repair
T-AK	Maritime prepositioning ship
T-AOT	Tankers
T-AKR	Roll-on/Roll-off

Class

Within a type classification of vessels there are *classes*. Ships belonging to a particular class are built from the same plans and are very much alike; in many cases, they are identical except for the different hull number painted on their bows. The first ship built of a class determines the name of the class. For example, after World War II the United States redesigned its aircraft carriers to accommodate the newly invented jet aircraft then entering the fleet. The first of these new aircraft carriers to be built was commissioned as USS *Forrestal* (CV 59). She was the fifty-ninth aircraft carrier, but the first of this new class. Satisfied with these new ships, the Navy built three more—USS *Saratoga* (CV 60), USS *Ranger* (CV 61), and USS *Independence* (CV 62)—all of which are referred to as *Forrestal*-class carriers.

Later, some major improvements were deemed necessary, so the Navy redesigned its aircraft carriers significantly enough that they were considered a new class of carrier. The first of these new and different carriers was named USS *Kitty Hawk* (CV 63), so the next ship built after her, USS *Constellation* (CV 64), was considered a *Kitty Hawk*–class aircraft carrier.

Ship Types and Their Missions

The many different types of vessels have specific functions. Some exist primarily to engage in combat with enemy forces (other vessels, aircraft, or land targets) and are generally referred to as *com-*

batants. Others exist to deliver the supplies (fuel, ammunition, food, and repair parts) needed to keep a ship operating and are generally referred to as *auxiliaries*. Still others, known as *amphibious* ships, are designed to take troops where they are needed and get them ashore.

Aircraft Carriers

These gigantic ships have been described as both the world's largest combatant ships and the world's smallest airfields. The various classes range in displacement between 75,000 and 96,000 tons and carry between seventy-five and eighty-five aircraft of various types. It requires more than 5,000 personnel to operate an aircraft carrier and her aircraft.

Aircraft carriers carry an assortment of aircraft capable of performing a wide variety of missions, including air support to troops ashore, bombardment missions, antisubmarine operations, rescue missions, reconnaissance, and antiair warfare. Because of their

USS *Abraham Lincoln* (CVN 72).   PH3 Greg Welch

powerful engines and four screws, carriers are capable of high speed, and they are capable of staying at sea for long periods of time, making them a potent weapon in a wide variety of scenarios. Some of the U.S. Navy's carriers are driven by oil-fired boilers; others, designated CVN, are nuclear powered.

Cruisers

These medium-sized (around 10,000 tons displacement) ships are particularly potent in antiair missions, but they are capable of a number of other missions as well, including antisurface and anti-submarine. They are equipped with missiles that can knock out incoming raids from enemy aircraft or missile attacks. With other specially designed missiles, they are able to hit land or sea targets at substantial distances.

Currently, the Navy's cruisers are all *Ticonderoga*-class (designated CG) ships, which are powered by gas turbines and equipped with the very sophisticated Aegis combat system. This integrated combat system is highly automated, exceptionally fast, and capable of conducting antiair, antisurface, and antisubmarine warfare simultaneously.

USS *Port Royal* (CG 73). U.S. Navy, Christopher Mobley

Destroyers

In today's Navy, destroyers perform a wide range of duties. They can serve as part of a screen unit in a carrier task group, protecting it from various forms of attack. They can detect and engage enemy submarines, aircraft, missiles, and surface ships. In an amphibious assault, a destroyer's weapons can help protect against enemy forces at sea and ashore. In short, destroyers have a well-deserved reputation of being the "workhorses" of the fleet.

Previous classes of destroyer were rather small—some displacing as little as 400 tons—but today's *Spruance*-class destroyers are 563 feet long and 55 feet in beam, displace 7,800 tons, and have a crew of 250. The *Spruance*s were the first major ships to be powered by gas turbines. Their 80,000-horsepower gas-turbine-drive engineering plants can go from "cold iron" (meaning no engines on the line) to full speed in twelve minutes. Their weaponry

USS *Fife* (DD 991).   U.S. Naval Institute

consists of torpedoes, guns, antisubmarine rockets, cruise missiles, and short-range antiair missiles.

The newer *Arleigh Burke* class, like the *Ticonderoga*-class cruisers, is equipped with the Aegis system, making it the most potent class of destroyer ever built. At one time, the differences between cruisers and destroyers were significant. Today, the differences are not so obvious.

USS *Higgins* (DDG 76).   U.S. Navy, Frederick McCahan

Frigates

The frigate first appeared in the U.S. Navy during World War II as the destroyer escort (DE). In 1975, these ships were re-designated as *frigates* (FF).

A number of classes have been built since then, but today the *Oliver Hazard Perry*–class frigates are the only ones in commission in the U.S. Navy. These ships carry crews of a little more than 200 and may be viewed as scaled-down destroyers. They protect amphibious forces, underway replenishment operations, and merchant-ship convoys.

Submarines

The Navy has two types of submarine: one is called *attack* and is designated SSN, while the other is called *fleet ballistic missile* and is designated SSBN. All U.S. submarines currently are nuclear powered.

The SSN's primary mission is to attack other submarines and ships, but they are also assigned secondary missions, which may include surveillance and reconnaissance, direct task-force support, landing-force support, land attack, mine laying, and rescue.

USS *Taylor* (FFG 50).   U.S. Naval Institute

The SSN's principal weapons are high-speed wire-guided torpedoes and cruise missiles for use against surface and land targets.

The SSBNs have a strategic mission, in that they are meant to deter or participate in a nuclear-missile exchange. Their highly sophisticated, very potent ballistic missiles are capable of hitting targets many thousands of miles away and causing tremendous destruction.

These vessels must remain submerged for long periods of time, virtually out of contact with the rest of the world, waiting to carry out a mission that could be devastating to the whole world. This is a stressful environment for the crews; to alleviate some of that stress, two separate crews operate SSBNs during alternate periods. One is called the blue crew and the other the gold crew. On return from an extended patrol, one crew relieves the other, and the ship returns to patrol following a brief period alongside her tender or in port. The relieved crew enters a monthlong period of rest, recreation, and leave that is followed by two months of training. This system allows each crew time ashore, while keeping the entire force of SSBNs cruising on deep patrol except for very brief periods.

USS *Cheyenne* (SSN 773).   U.S. Navy

USS *Maine* (SSBN 741).   PH1 Michael J. Rinaldi

Patrol Combatants

Some smaller coastal and riverine craft are also in service. Among
the more prevalent types are the coastal patrol ships of the *Cyclone*
(PC 1) class. Measuring 170 feet long, with a 35-knot speed and
armed with two 25-mm guns, Stinger missiles, and lighter weapons,
the *Cyclones* are used for special warfare and coastal interdiction
missions.

Mine-Warfare Ships

The U.S. Navy currently uses two types of mine-warfare vessel.
The *Osprey* (MHC 51)-class designation is for minehunters, and
the *Avenger* (MCM 1)-class ships are mine-countermeasures
ships. The MHCs specialize in detecting and locating today's
highly sophisticated mine; the MCMs are tasked with removing or
destroying them.

Amphibious Warfare Ships

Often referred to as the "amphibs" or "gators," these ships work
mainly where sea and land meet, and where Navy–Marine Corps
teams carry out assault landings. Such operations call for a variety
of types of ships. Many are transports of varied designs, used to

USS *Chinook* (PC 9).   U.S. Navy, William F. Gowdy

sealift Marines and their equipment from bases to landing beaches. The differences lie in ship design and the way troops and their gear are moved from ship to shore, which can be done by means of landing craft, helicopters, or tracked amphibious vehicles.

Dock-landing ship (LSD). These ships have a well deck inside the vessel that can be flooded so that waterborne landing craft and

USS *Osprey* (MHC 51).   Intermarine, USA

USS *Pearl Harbor* (LSD 52).   U.S. Navy, Mahlon K. Miller

vehicles can be floated out of the ship's stern gate. They also have a limited capacity for handling troop-carrying helicopters.

Amphibious transport dock (LPD). These ships are similar to the LSD in that they deliver troops and equipment in landing craft or vehicles carried in a well deck and floated out through a stern gate, but their helicopter capacity is more extensive.

General-purpose assault ship (LHA). Of all the ship types discussed so far, only aircraft carriers are larger than these. The five ships of the *Tarawa* (LHA 1) class displace more than 39,000 tons. They resemble aircraft carriers and are capable of simultaneous helicopter and landing-craft operations, for they have both flight and well decks.

Multipurpose-assault ship (LHD). These large ships resemble the LHA but incorporate many changes as a result of experience with the *Tarawa* class. LHDs operate air-cushion landing craft (LCACs) and heavy helicopters. They function as sea-control ships, when necessary, by operating antisubmarine helicopters and AV-8B Harrier vertical/short takeoff and landing (V/STOL) airplanes.

Amphibious command ship (LCC). LCCs serve as floating command centers, providing control and communication facilities for embarked sea, air, and land commanders and their staffs.

Pre-commissioning Unit *San Antonio* (LPD 17).   Northrop Grumman Corporation

USS *Tarawa* (LHA 1).   U.S. Navy, Taylor Goode

USS *Wasp* (LHD 1).   U.S. Navy

Underway-Replenishment Ships

If they are going to be combat-effective, warships must be able to remain at sea for weeks at a time with fuel, provisions, parts, and ammunition. The U.S. Navy is highly proficient at underway replenishment (UNREP) techniques that use special cargo-handling

Landing Craft Air Cushion (LCAC).   U.S. Navy, Ted Banks

USS *Mount Whitney* (LCC 20).   U.S. Naval Institute

gear to make transfers from one ship to another while the two are steaming abreast or, in some cases, astern. Vertical replenishment (VERTREP) is a form of UNREP in which cargo-carrying helicopters are used to transfer goods from one ship to another. MSC ships (such as T-AOs and T-AEs) carry out much of the UNREP capability of the Navy today, but *fast combat–support ships (AOEs)* are the largest and most powerful of the Navy's noncombatant seagoing units. Because of their high-speed capability, these 50,000-ton seagoing warehouses are capable of operating with fast task forces. AOEs carry fuel, ammunition, and stores.

Fleet Support Ships

UNREP vessels are only one type of the auxiliaries that help carry out the Navy's many missions. A number of other ships play vital roles in keeping the fleet operating at peak efficiency.

Tenders. Submarine tenders (ASs) and destroyer tenders (ADs) are full of maintenance and repair shops and are manned by technicians with a wide variety of skills so that vessels coming alongside can receive rather extensive repairs or have major maintenance performed on them.

Salvage vessels. Rescue, salvage, and towing ships (ARSs) provide rapid firefighting, dewatering, battle-damage repair, and towing assistance to save ships that have been in battle or victims

USNS *Yukon* (T-AO 202).   U.S. Navy, Jason T. Poplin

of some other disaster from further loss or damage. Equipped with specialized equipment and manned by salvage divers, these ships can also perform rescue and salvage operations underwater.

Command Ships (AGF)

Two former amphibious ships have been converted into command ships to serve in a command-and-communications role in the Middle East. They are painted white to help their air conditioners cope with the intense heat of the region. They are equipped with a great deal of highly sophisticated sensors and communications systems.

Service Craft

Also among the Navy's waterborne resources is a large and varied group of service craft. Some are huge vessels like the large auxiliary floating dry docks that can take very large vessels aboard and raise them out of the water for repairs. Barracks craft accommodate crews when their ships are being overhauled or repaired. Lighters are barges used to store and transport materials and to house pier-side repair shops. Some gasoline barges, fuel-oil barges, and water barges are self-propelled; those that are not depend on tugs. Floating cranes and wrecking derricks are towed from place to place as needed. Diving tenders support diving operations, and ferryboats or launches, which carry people, automobiles, and equipment, are usually located at Navy bases where facilities are spread out over large distances. Best known of the service craft are the harbor tugs, large and small, that aid ships in docking and undocking, provide firefighting services when needed, perform rescues, and haul lighters from place to place.

Aircraft of the U.S. Navy   13

Naval aircraft are an essential component of sea power. The U.S. Navy has thousands of aircraft in its inventory that perform a wide variety of missions, many from the decks of ships and others from naval air stations. The many kinds of fixed-wing and rotary-wing (helicopter) aircraft flown by the Navy include fighters, attack, combined fighter-attack, antisubmarine, patrol, early warning, general utility, in-flight refueling, transport, and trainers. Naval aircraft are organized into *squadrons* and these are further grouped into *air wings*.

Basic Aircraft Nomenclature

Because aircraft are such an important component of the Navy, you should be familiar with certain basic terms concerning the structure of airplanes and helicopters.

The *fuselage* is the main body of the aircraft. The *wings* are strong structural members attached to the fuselage. Their airfoil shape provides the lift that supports the plane in flight. Wings are fitted with flaps for increased lift and may carry fuel tanks, guns, rockets, missiles, and other weapons, engines, and landing gear. Instead of having wings in the traditional sense, helicopters have rotors (which are actually wings that rotate).

The *tail assembly* of a fixed-wing aircraft consists of vertical and horizontal stabilizers, rudder(s), and elevators. These components are key elements in the flight controls of the aircraft.

The *landing gear* usually means the wheels, but in certain aircraft skids, skis, or floats may replace the wheels.

The *power plant* develops the thrust or force that propels the aircraft forward, providing mobility and (in combination with the wings) the lift necessary to keep the aircraft aloft. In the case of

The following material is extracted from *The Bluejacket's Manual*, Centennial Edition (Annapolis, Md.: Naval Institute Press, 2002).

helicopters, the power plant provides the power to keep the rotors spinning, which keeps the aircraft aloft and allows it to hover as well as move through the air. The power plant may consist of reciprocating (piston) engines that drive propellers, jet engines that develop thrust (turbojet and turbofan), or turbine engines and propellers or rotors in combination (turboprop or turbo shaft).

Another useful term is *Mach,* which is commonly used to measure the speed capability of an aircraft or missile. Formally defined as the ratio of speed of an object to the speed of sound in the surrounding atmosphere, it is used as follows. An aircraft traveling at Mach 1 would be moving at the speed of sound. One going Mach 2 would be going twice the speed of sound, and Mach 1.5 would be one-and-a-half times the speed of sound. Depending upon the altitude, temperature, and some other variables, the speed of sound varies, but a rough figure to use for approximation is 650 miles per hour. So an aircraft flying at Mach 2 would be moving at a speed of *approximately* 1,300 miles per hour. An aircraft that is able to fly faster than the speed of sound (Mach 1) is said to be *supersonic* and one than cannot is called *subsonic.*

Aircraft Designations

Many types, designs, and modifications of aircraft form the naval air arm of the Navy. Like ships, aircraft have names, usually chosen by the designers or developers and approved by the Navy. For example, one type of the Navy's combat aircraft is named "Hornet," while the Navy's most prevalent patrol aircraft are known as "Orions." A more revealing system of letters and numbers (aircraft designations) is used to distinguish among the many types and variations of naval aircraft in service. Both the names and the designations are applied to all aircraft of a given type; individual aircraft are identified with a unique number.

The aircraft designation is a letter/number combination that tells you certain basic facts about the aircraft. All the various letter/number combinations can be confusing to the uninitiated, but it helps to remember that the one thing common to all aircraft designations is the hyphen. Where the various letters and numbers are placed in relation to the hyphen will help you keep their intended meaning clear in your mind. "F-14," for example, indicates a Tomcat fighter plane. The *F* before the hyphen represents the *basic mission* (or *type*) of the aircraft and stands for "fighter." The

"14" following the hyphen is the *design number.* To reduce confusion, these designations are used by all the U.S. armed forces so an
F-14 in the Air Force means the same thing as an F-14 in the
Navy. One other thing to keep in mind (to avoid confusion) is that
this system has not always been in effect; earlier in aviation history other designation systems were used, so if you are reading
about aircraft in World War II, for example, the aircraft designations will not be the same.

Basic Mission and Type Symbols

A	Attack
B	Bomber
C	Cargo/ transport
E	Special electronics installation
F	Fighter
H	Helicopter
O	Observation
P	Patrol
S	Antisubmarine
T	Trainer
U	Utility
V	V/STOL (Vertical/short takeoff and landing)

Future modifications to the F-14 would call for a *series symbol,*
which would indicate an improvement of or a major change to the
same design. This symbol is placed after the design number. The
first such change would cause the aircraft to be called an "F-14A,"
the next major modification would result in an "F-14B," and so on.

When the basic mission of an airplane has been considerably
modified, a *modified-mission symbol* is added before the original
basic mission symbol. For example, an F-14C modified to act primarily as a reconnaissance plane would become an "RF-14C."

Modified-Mission Symbols

C	Transport
D	Director
H	Search/rescue
K	Tanker
L	Cold weather

M	Mine countermeasures
O	Observation
Q	Drone
R	Reconnaissance
V	Staff transport
W	Weather reconnaissance

Finally, there is the *special-use symbol,* a letter prefix indicating that the aircraft is being used for special work and experimentation, or that it is in planning or is a prototype.

Consider our imaginary RF-14C. If it were to be used as an experimental aircraft to test some new design modification, it would have an *X* added to the designation and become an XRF-14C. Despite this, the basic airplane is still the F-14, and most Navy personnel would recognize it as such despite its changes. To avoid confusion, these special-use symbols are different from other letters used in aircraft designations.

Special-Use Symbols

J	Special test, temporary (after test, aircraft will be returned to its original configuration)
N	Special test, permanent (aircraft has been too drastically altered for testing to permit returning it to its original configuration)
X	Experimental (developmental stage in which basic mission has not been established)
Y	Prototype (only a few procured for development of design)
Z	Planning (used for identification during planning)

Types of Naval Aircraft

There are many different types of aircraft in the U.S. Navy's inventory. Some of these were designed specifically for naval use, but many are used by the other armed forces as well. Some are fixed-wing while others are helicopters.

Fighters

The primary function of fighters is to destroy other aircraft and incoming missiles. They are the aircraft you would normally see involved in a "dogfight." Fighters are very fast and highly maneuverable. They intercept and engage enemy aircraft, defend surface forces, escort other kinds of aircraft when they are carrying out their missions in hostile areas, and support ground troops.

The Navy currently operates two types of fighter aircraft. The **F-14 Tomcat** is a twin-engine, variable-sweep-wing (meaning that the wings can be swept backward or forward depending on what the pilot is trying to accomplish), all-weather fighter-interceptor. It has a powerful gun system and fires air-to-air missiles to destroy enemy aircraft. The aircraft's sophisticated radar/missile combination enables it to track twenty-four targets simultaneously and attack six with missiles while continuing to scan the airspace. It can select and destroy targets up to a hundred miles away. The F-14D has improved computerization, radar, communications and electronics, and weaponry. It can fly at Mach 1.88 and has a range of nearly 2,000 miles without refueling (less when involved in high-speed maneuvering).

The **F/A-18** Hornet is designed to carry out *two* missions: the *F* stands for *fighter* and the *A* for *attack*. This is a supersonic twin-engine jet that can carry a variety of armament depending upon the

F-14 Tomcat.   U.S. Navy, Paul Farley

mission, including various missiles, rockets, and bombs. It has an effective combat radius of several hundred miles and can fly in virtually all weather conditions.

A newer, more capable variation of the Hornet is the **Super Hornet.** It has replaced the F-14 Tomcat as the primary fighter aircraft on carriers.

Attack

The attack aircraft's main job is to destroy enemy targets, at sea and ashore, with rockets, guided missiles, torpedoes, mines, and bombs. As already mentioned, the F/A-18 Hornet performs this role for the Navy. The **AV-8B Harrier** also serves as an attack aircraft. Its vertical landing and takeoff ability means it does not need a runway (or even a full-length aircraft carrier flight deck) to function, which makes it particularly well suited for ground combat-support operations. A light-attack, single-engine aircraft, it is flown by Marine Corps pilots from shore sites or amphibious assault ships. The Harrier's armament includes cluster, general-purpose, and laser-guided bombs, as well as rockets, missiles, and guns.

F/A-18C Hornet.   U.S. Navy, Greg E. Badger

F/A-18 Super Hornet.   U.S. Navy, Christopher L. Jordan

Patrol

These large airplanes, with lower speeds but very long flying range, have the primary mission of antisubmarine patrol. They also can be used to drop mines or bombs and can fire missiles. They have infrared, acoustic, and magnetic-detection devices for finding and tracking submarines. The **P-3C Orion** is a propeller-driven, land-based, long-range, over-water antisubmarine patrol plane. Since the prototype first flew in 1958, the P-3 has undergone many improvements and continues to play a major antisubmarine role for the Navy. The P-3 flies with a normal crew of ten (pilots, flight engineers, sensor operators, and in-flight technicians). It has a maximum speed of 473 mph but normally cruises at 377 mph. Its maximum mission radius is more than 2,000 miles.

Antisubmarine

Searching out submarines visually, by radar and magnetic detection, or by signals sent from floating sonobuoys, these aircraft attack with rockets, depth charges, or homing torpedoes.

The P-3 Orion (see above) is a land-based antisubmarine aircraft, but the **S-3 Viking** is carrier based. A subsonic, all-weather, long-range, high-endurance, turbofan-powered aircraft, the Viking can locate and destroy enemy submarines, including newer high-

AV-8B Harrier. U.S. Navy

speed, deep-submergence, quiet versions. With a crew of four, the Viking can operate independently or in tandem with long-range, land-based antisubmarine units, such as the P-3. Weapons carried by the S-3 include various combinations of torpedoes, depth charges, missiles, rockets, and special weapons.

P-3C Orion patrol aircraft.   U.S. Naval Institute

S-3B Viking.   U.S. Navy, Kristi J. Earl

The **SH-60B Seahawk** is a helicopter designed to operate from surface ships to increase their antisubmarine capability. The SH-60F version is designed to operate from aircraft carriers for the same purpose. These sophisticated helicopters employ a long-range dipping sonar in addition to dropping sonobuoys to track submarines. They are capable of attacking as well as detecting enemy submarines. The HH-60H version is deployed on board aircraft carriers and is used for search and rescue (SAR) operations. The MH-60R version will eventually replace both the SH-60B and SH-60F.

Mine Warfare

Helicopters are particularly well suited for both laying and sweeping mines. The **MH-53E Sea Dragon** is used on CVs, LPDs, LHDs, and LHAs for minesweeping, mine neutralization, mine spotting, floating mine destruction, and channel marking.

Command and Control

Maintaining communications is absolutely vital in modern warfare. The land-based **E-6A Mercury** is used in conjunction with

SH-60B Seahawk, armed with AGM-119 Penguin antiship missile.
U.S. Navy, Edward G. Martens

MH-60R Knighthawk.   U.S. Navy

MH-53E Sea Dragon with USS *Gettysburg* (CG 64) and USS *Philippine Sea* (CG 58).   U.S. Navy, Rob Gaston

ballistic-missile submarines to ensure a viable strategic deterrence role. The **E-2C Hawkeye** is a carrier-based, propeller-driven aircraft that provides airborne early warning, threat analysis, and air-control functions for carrier battle groups. By flying high above the battle group, the E-2 uses its powerful radar system to watch over and control a much larger area than could be covered by shipboard radar systems. Its sophisticated communications systems help to control the employment of the aircraft sent aloft by the carrier.

Electronic Warfare

The **EA-6B Prowler,** the first Navy plane designed and built specifically for tactical electronic warfare, is an all-weather, four-seat, subsonic, carrier-based plane. It is the most advanced airborne electronic-warfare aircraft in existence. Its missions include the jamming of enemy electronic signals to render them incapable of performing; such a capability thereby provides a significant tactical advantage.

The **EP-3E Orion (Aries II)** is an electronic surveillance version of the P-3 Orion. Operating from land bases and using the highly sophisticated Aries II surveillance system, this aircraft is capable of collecting valuable electronic data from real or potential enemies while remaining in international airspace.

E-2C Hawkeye.   U.S. Navy, Jim Hampshire

EA-6B Prowler.   U.S. Navy, Victor Dymond

Transport

Transport planes carry cargo and personnel. Some are land based and others can be operated from aircraft carriers.

The **C-9B Skytrain II** is a Navy version of the commercial DC-9 series airliner that can carry a significant payload of cargo or passengers.

The **C-130 Hercules** was originally a transport aircraft for personnel, weapons, and supplies for all the services, but the Navy uses this four-engine turboprop aircraft for a variety of roles. As an EC-130, it is an electronic surveillance aircraft. As a KC-130, it is used for aerial refueling of tactical aircraft from jets to helicopters. Probably the most versatile tactical-transport aircraft ever built, the Hercules is also used in search and rescue missions, in space-capsule recovery, for landings (with skis) on snow and ice, and for special cargo delivery. It has even landed and taken off from a carrier deck without the benefit of arresting gear or catapults.

The **C-2A Greyhound,** a twin turboprop aircraft, has the primary mission of transporting people and cargo to and from aircraft carriers (called "carrier on-board delivery"—COD). The Greyhound provides critical support between shore facilities and air-

C-9B Skytrain.   U.S. Naval Institute

craft carriers deployed throughout the world. Its cabin can be readily configured to accommodate cargo, passengers, or a combination of both. It is used for transporting personnel, mail, key logistics items, such mission-essential cargo as jet engines, and litter patients for medical evacuation.

C-2A Greyhound.   U.S. Navy, Aaron Peterson

The **CH-46 Sea Knight** serves as a vertical-replenishment helicopter in the fleet, meaning that it is used to lift cargo from one ship and place it on another while the ships are under way. It has a crew of three and can carry approximately 6,000 pounds of cargo in a sling beneath the fuselage. The MH-60S, a cargo variant of the SH-60, will replace the CH-64.

The **CH-53 Sea Stallion** transports supplies, equipment, and personnel. It is useful for personnel evacuations or can be used to insert troops where needed. It can carry thirty-seven fully equipped troops, twenty-four litter patients plus four attendants, or 8,000 pounds of cargo.

The **CH-53E Super Stallion** is the largest and most powerful helicopter in production. Despite its large size, it is shipboard compatible and configured for the lift and movement of cargo, passengers, and heavy, oversized equipment. It can move large quantities of cargo, transfer damaged aircraft or vehicles, provide mobile-construction support, move nuclear weapons, and participate in various mine-warfare missions.

Trainer

Trainers are generally two-seat airplanes that allow instructors and students to go aloft together to learn or perfect the techniques of

HH-46D Sea Knight.   U.S. Navy, Aida E. Miranda

CH-53D Sea Stallion.   U.S. Navy, Robert M. Schalk

CH-53E Super Stallion.   U.S. Navy, Jeffrey Truett

flying. Although several types of trainers are in use, the most sophisticated type is the **T-45A Goshawk,** which is used in the training of prospective tactical Navy and Marine Corps jet pilots.

Aircraft Squadrons

Naval aircraft are organized into squadrons for administrative and operational purposes. Some squadrons are carrier based, spending part of their time on board aircraft carriers. Others are land based and, if their mission requires it, periodically deploy to other locations. Some squadrons are subdivided into detachments and are scattered to ships or various bases.

Squadrons are identified by letter-number designations that, like ship hull numbers, tell something about their mission while giving them a unique identity. The first letter in a squadron designation is either a *V* or an *H*. The latter is used for squadrons made up entirely of helicopters. *V* indicates fixed-wing aircraft. If a squadron has both helicopters and fixed-wing aircraft, it is designated by a *V*. In the days when there was a third type of aircraft, the lighter-than-air (or dirigible) type, those squadrons were designated by a *Z*. The letter(s) following the *V* or *H* indicate the squadron's mission(s). For example, a squadron whose primary purpose is training pilots to fly fixed-wing aircraft would be designated "VT." By adding a number, an individual squadron takes on a unique identity; for example, "VT-3." The numbers, in most cases, have some logic to them—such as even numbers indicating Atlantic Fleet squadrons and odd numbers designating Pacific Fleet—but movement and the periodic establishment and disestablishment of various squadrons have clouded some of the original intended logic.

Aircraft Squadron Designations

HC	Helicopter combat support
HCS	Helicopter combat-support special
HM	Helicopter mine countermeasures
HS	Helicopter antisubmarine
HSL	Light helicopter antisubmarine
HT	Helicopter training
VA	Attack
VAQ	Tactical electronic warfare

VAW	Carrier airborne early warning
VC	Fleet composite
VF	Fighter
VFA	Strike fighter
VFC	Fighter composite
VP	Patrol
VQ	Reconnaissance/strategic communications
VR	Fleet logistics support
VRC	Carrier logistics support
VS	Sea control (antisubmarine warfare, etc.)
VT	Training
VX	Test and evaluation

Air Wings

Aircraft squadrons are typically grouped into larger organizational units called *air wings*. A carrier air wing (CVW) is usually made up of about eight squadrons, each serving a different but integrated purpose. With these various squadrons on board, an aircraft carrier can carry out a wide variety of missions. Table 13.1 shows a typical carrier air wing.

Table 13.1 Typical Carrier Air Wing

Squadron	Function	Type	Aircraft Number
VF	Fighter	F-14	14
VFA	Strike Fighter	F/A-18	12
VAW	Early Warning	E-2	4
VAQ	Electronic Warfare	EA-6B	4
VS	Sea Control	S-3	8
HS	Antisubmarine/Rescue	SH-60	8
VRC[a]	Carrier Logistics	C-2	2

[a]Detachment

Weapon Systems of the U.S. Navy

14

The Navy's overall mission is to maintain sufficient military capability to effectively deter a would-be enemy from using military power against the United States and its allies, to defend against any attacks that might occur, and to take offensive action against the enemy once hostilities have begun. Weapons are the mainstay of the military. Without them, the Navy could not carry out its combat missions or defend its ships, planes, bases, and personnel.

To understand the weapons used by the Navy, one should first be familiar with the following terms.

Ordnance. This term applies to the various components associated with a ship's or aircraft's firepower: guns, gun mounts, turrets, ammunition, guided missiles, rockets, and units that control and support these weapons.

Weapon system. When a number of ordnance components are integrated so as to find, track, and deliver fire onto a target, this is called a weapon system. For example, a gun would be called a weapon, but the gun plus the radars used to find and track the target and the ammunition-handling equipment used to load it would be called a weapon system.

Gun. In its most basic form, a gun is a tube closed at one end from which a projectile is propelled by the burning of gunpowder. A projectile (bullet) fired from a gun gets all of its traveling energy at the instant it is fired (unlike rockets and missiles whose burning fuels continue to propel them through the air).

Rocket. A weapon containing a propulsion section to propel the weapon through the air and an explosive section used to do damage to an enemy. A rocket is unable to change its direction of movement after it has been fired.

The following material is extracted from *The Bluejacket's Manual,* Centennial Edition (Annapolis, Md.: Naval Institute Press, 2002).

Missile. Originally called a "*guided* missile," this weapon is essentially a rocket (that is, it has a propulsion section and an explosive section), but it also has a *guidance* section that allows its direction to be changed in mid-flight in order to better hit the target.

Torpedo. A self-propelled underwater weapon used against surface and underwater targets. Some torpedoes function like underwater rockets in that they cannot be controlled once they have been launched, while other, more sophisticated versions can be guided, like an airborne missile, after they have been launched.

Mine. An underwater explosive weapon put into position by surface ships, submarines, or aircraft. A mine explodes only when a target comes near or into contact with it.

Depth charge. Antisubmarine weapons fired or dropped by a ship or aircraft, and set to explode either at a certain depth or in proximity to a submarine.

Bomb. Any weapon—other than a torpedo, mine, rocket, or missile—that is dropped from an aircraft. Bombs are free-fall (that is, they have no propulsion power to deliver them to the target) explosive weapons and may be either "dumb" (unguided) or "smart" (with a guidance system to steer them to their target).

Missiles and Rockets

The Navy has a great many missiles and some rockets in its weapons inventory. The chief advantage of rockets and missiles over gun and bomb systems is their extended range. Rockets and missiles can be fired from either ships (including submarines) or aircraft. Missiles, of course, are more effective than rockets because of their increased accuracy. The major disadvantage of these weapons is their added cost.

Rocket and Missile Components

Rockets have three major components—the airframe, the power plant, and the warhead. As has been explained, missiles have a fourth component—the guidance system.

The airframe is the body of the rocket or missile, which determines its flight characteristics and contains the other components. It must be light because the other parts are heavy. Airframes are made of aluminum alloys, magnesium, and high-tensile (high-stress) steel. These metals can withstand extreme heat and pressure.

The power plant is similar to the engines of an aircraft except that the latter are reusable while the missile's propulsion unit is expended in its one flight. The power plant must propel the rocket or missile at very high speeds to minimize its chance of being shot down before reaching its intended target. Some must be able to operate at very high altitudes where there is little or no atmosphere, and therefore are required to carry both the fuel and an oxidizer in order to sustain combustion. Other, less expensive power plants are air-breathing plants that carry only the fuel, but they cannot operate above about 70,000 feet.

The warhead is the part that does the damage. Its explosive may be conventional or nuclear.

Missile Guidance Systems

The guidance system in missiles constantly corrects the flight path until it intercepts the target. There are four different types of guidance systems: inertial, homing, command, or beam riding. Many missiles use a combination of two of these systems—one guiding the missile through the middle course and the other used during the terminal stage.

Inertial Guidance

This type of guidance uses a predetermined path programmed into an onboard missile computer before launch. Missile speed and direction are checked constantly, and the computer makes corrections to keep it on course.

Homing Guidance

In this type of guidance, the missile picks up and tracks a target by radar, optical devices, or heat-seeking methods.

In an *active* homing system, the missile itself emits a signal that is reflected off the target and picked up by a receiver in the missile.

In a *semi-active* homing system, the signal comes from the launching ship or plane rather than from the missile itself and is then received by the missile, which uses the information received to correct its flight.

A *passive* homing system does not require either the missile or the firing ship or aircraft to emit a signal, but uses the *target*'s emissions to home in on. For example, some passive homers use a target's own radar signals to home on; a heat-seeking missile can home in on the heat put out by the target's engines.

Command Guidance

After the missile is launched on an intercept course, a computer evaluates how it is doing in relation to the target and transmits orders to the missile to change its track as necessary to ensure that it hits the target.

Beam-Riding Guidance

The missile follows a radar beam to the target. A computer in the missile keeps it centered within the radar beam. Several missiles may ride the same beam simultaneously. If the missile wanders outside the beam, it will automatically destroy itself.

Missile and Rocket Designations

Navy rockets and missiles are often identified by a three-letter designation, followed by a number. For example, the Sparrow missile is known as an AIM-7. The *A* tells you that the missile is launched from an airplane. If the first letter is an *R,* it means the missile is launched from a ship; *U* means that it is submarine launched.

The second letter tells you the mission. *I* indicates air intercept (shoots down other aircraft), *G* means surface attack (ships or land targets), and *U* means the target is a submarine.

The third letter is either *R* (for rocket) or *M* (for missile).

The number(s) used differentiate between one similar system and another and represent the sequential development of the missile; for example, the first missile of a particular type that was developed was designated number *1* and the next was number *2,* and so on.

Missile Categories

Missiles can be launched from aircraft, ships, and submarines; depending upon their intended target, they may be categorized as air-to-air, air-to-surface, surface-to-air, and so on. Some missiles can be used against air and surface targets alike.

Air-to-Air

Carried by naval aircraft to shoot down enemy aircraft, some of the current ones in use are listed below.

Sparrow. Designated the AIM-7, this highly maneuverable radar-guided missile can attack enemy aircraft from any direction in virtually all weather conditions and has a range of more than thirty nautical miles.

Sidewinder. The AIM-9 is an all-weather heat-seeking missile with a range of five to ten nautical miles depending upon conditions.

Phoenix. The AIM-54 is a highly sophisticated, radar-guided, long-range (more than a hundred miles) missile that is fired only by the F-14 Tomcat fighter aircraft.

AMRAAM. The AIM-120 is a radar-guided sophisticated missile with a range of approximately thirty miles. "AMRAAM" stands for advanced medium-range air-to-air missile.

Air-to-Ground
Despite the name, these missiles can be used against ships at sea as well as inland targets.

Shrike. Designated AGM-45, this missile is delivered by fighter aircraft and is designed to home in on enemy antiaircraft radars.

HARM. The AGM-88 is named for its capabilities as a "high-speed antiradiation missile." It homes in on enemy radar-equipped air defense systems.

Maverick. The AGM-65 is an infrared-guided missile designed for day or night sea warfare (antiship) and land interdiction missions.

Surface-to-Air
Designed to shoot down incoming enemy aircraft and missiles, these weapons can be used in concert with or instead of friendly interceptor aircraft.

F/A-18 Hornet.   Hughes Aircraft Company

Standard. The missiles currently in use by the Navy are grouped together in several variations of what are called the Standard (RIM-66) missiles. The SM-1 MR (medium range) and SM-2 MR are two common variations. There is also an extended range version that is designated "ER" instead of "MR."

Sea-Sparrow. Ships having no standard missile capabilities carry a modified version of the Sparrow air-to-air missile. This missile has a range of about ten nautical miles and is designed to provide close-in protection when other means of antiair defense have been ineffective.

Cruise Missiles

These missiles can be fired from surface ships to strike other surface ships and could therefore be called surface-to-surface missiles, but because they may also be fired from submarines or from aircraft to hit surface targets, they are more generically referred to as cruise missiles.

Harpoon. Because Harpoons can be fired from virtually every combatant in the Navy (surface ships, submarines, and aircraft) the Harpoon is designated as the RGM-84, the UGM-84, and the AGM-84. It has a range of seventy-five-plus miles and a version called SLAM (for standoff land attack missile) is used to attack land targets.

Tomahawk. The BGM-109 can be used in several variations, including a TASM (Tomahawk antiship missile), a TLAM (Tomahawk land-attack missile), and a TLAM(N) (nuclear) version. These missiles vary in range from 250-plus nautical miles in the TASM version to 750-plus nautical miles and 1,200-plus nautical miles in the TLAM and TLAM(N) versions, respectively.

Fleet Ballistic Missiles

With nuclear warheads capable of hitting multiple targets and doing massive damage, these missiles are designed for strategic deterrence and attack. They represent some of the greatest advances in modern weapons technology and can be launched from submerged submarines over a wide range of the earth.

Trident. These subsurface-to-surface missiles, in their most advanced version, the *Trident II,* have a range of more than 6,000 miles and are capable of carrying up to eight independent thermonuclear warheads.

Harpoon (RGM 8).   U.S. Naval Institute

Missile Launching Systems

Earlier missile systems had "dedicated" launchers—separate magazine-loaded launchers for each type of missile. This took up valuable space on board ship and increased topside weight. Later launchers handled more than one type of missile, but still had to be individually loaded. The newest launcher is the Mark 41 VLS (vertical launch system), used in the *Ticonderoga, Arleigh Burke,*

Trident missiles.　U.S. Naval Institute

and *Spruance* classes. Missiles are carried in below-deck ready-to-launch tubes; any needed mix of missiles can be fired right from these tubes in quick succession without the delays involved in reloading topside launchers.

Bombs

Bombs have four chief parts. The *case* is normally made of steel and contains the explosive. The *fuze* causes the bomb to explode when desired. The *fin* or *tail assembly* stabilizes the bomb during flight. The *arming-wire* assembly keeps the fuze(s) from being armed until after the bomb is dropped.

Bombs are classed as explosive, chemical, or practice. *General-purpose* (GP) bombs, weighing 100–2,000 pounds, are explosive-type bombs and are generally used against unarmored ships or ground targets for blast or fragmentation. *Semi-armor-piercing* (SAP) bombs are used against targets that are sufficiently protected so as to require the bomb to have some penetration capability in order to be effective. *Fragmentation* bombs are usually smaller explosives dropped in clusters against troops and ground targets.

Chemical bombs contain specialized chemical agents that are used for a specific purpose. They can contain chemicals—such as mustard gas, phosgene, tear gas, or vomiting gas—that are designed to disable or kill enemy personnel, or they can be smoke bombs that contain white phosphorus that ignites during the explosion and spreads heavy smoke over the target area in order to conceal movements of ships or troops. *Incendiary* bombs are a form of chemical bomb that produces intense fire when ignited and are used against troops and ground targets.

Practice and drill bombs used in training may be loaded with sand or water but are inert (carry no explosive) and will cause no damage other than simple impact.

Torpedoes

The torpedo is a self-propelled, explosive-carrying underwater weapon. Early torpedoes were basically of the "point-and-shoot" variety, but modern versions have some sort of guidance system that markedly increases the accuracy of the weapon.

A torpedo consists of a tail, afterbody, midsection, and head. The tail section includes the screws, fins, and control surfaces. The propulsion system is contained in the afterbody. The midsection houses batteries, compressed air, or liquid fuel. The head contains the explosive charge, fuze, and any acoustic or magnetic sensing devices.

Torpedo guidance systems are preset, wire guided, or homing. Preset torpedoes follow a set course and depth after they are launched. Wire-guided torpedoes have a thin wire connecting the torpedo and the firing vessel, through which guidance signals can be transmitted to the torpedo to direct it to intercept the target. Homing torpedoes are active, passive, or a combination of active/

passive. The active versions depend on the sensing signals generated and returned to the torpedo through a sonar device inside the torpedo. Passive types pick up telltale signals (such as noise or magnetic disturbances) to home in on. In the active/passive mode, the torpedo searches passively until a target is acquired, then active terminal guiding finishes the target destruction.

Surface ships launch torpedoes from tubes mounted topside, or propel them to the target area with a rocket called an antisubmarine rocket (ASROC). Submarines launch torpedoes through specially designed tubes, and aircraft deploy their torpedoes by parachute so as to reduce the impact when the weapon strikes the water.

Mines

Mines are passive weapons that are planted under the water to await the passage of enemy vessels to explode and do damage. Their advantage is that they operate independently (that is, no personnel are required to operate them once they have been planted). Their chief disadvantage is that they are indiscriminate (they can damage friendly or neutral vessels as well as enemy ones if precautions are not taken). You might be confused a bit if you read naval history and see the word "torpedo" used. In earlier times, what we now call a mine was called a torpedo.

Mines can be classified according to the method of actuation (firing), the method of planting, and their position in the water.

Mines may be actuated by contact and/or influence. A contact mine fires when a ship strikes it. Influence mines may be actuated by the underwater sound generated in a passing ship's current, by the ship's magnetic field, or by the mine's sensitivity to reduced water pressure caused by a passing ship.

Mines may be planted by surface craft, submarines, and aircraft. Planting mines using surface craft is the most dangerous method because the ship doing the planting is vulnerable to attack. Submarines can plant mines more secretly; aircraft are able to plant mines quickly and with less risk.

Moored contact mines are anchored in place and float near the surface of the water where a ship might strike them. Bottom mines, which lie on the ocean floor, are used only in relatively shallow water. They are influence mines, set off by sound, magnetism, or pressure.

There also exists a class of mine that contains a torpedo. When triggered, this torpedo is activated and homes in on the target.

Naval Guns

Guns have been a major component of naval armament for centuries. Early guns were highly inaccurate, often very dangerous devices that had to be loaded from the front end and aimed simply by pointing at a visible enemy. Today's guns are much more powerful and accurate, far safer, and aimed and controlled by sophisticated electronic and hydraulic systems.

Early cannons had smooth bores (inside the barrel) and usually fired round shot. Modern guns have *rifling* in their barrels, which is a network of ridges (called *lands*) and grooves shaped in a spiral

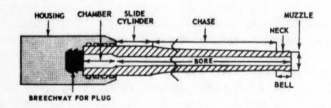

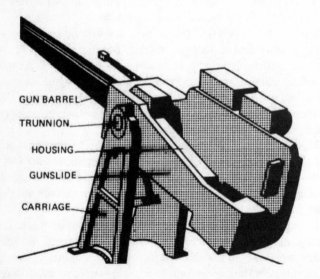

Some of the parts of a typical (simplified) naval gun.

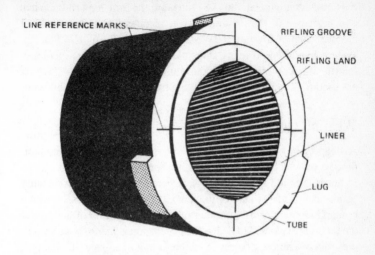

A view into the barrel of a naval gun shows the spiraling lands and grooves known as rifling.

that causes an elongated projectile to spin on its long axis (much as a well-thrown football does). This increases the range and accuracy of the gun.

Guns are not nearly as important to naval ships as they once were. Sophisticated missile systems, with their greater range and superior accuracy, have taken the place of the gun as the mainstay of naval armament. There is still a need for naval guns, however. Certain missions are accomplished more effectively through the use of guns, and they tend to be less expensive than missiles.

U.S. Navy guns are classified by their inside barrel diameter and by their barrel length. These two figures are expressed in a rather cryptic manner that may seem confusing at first, but makes sense once you understand what the figures are telling you. The first figure in a Navy gun classification is the inside barrel diameter, expressed in inches or millimeters (mm). The second part follows a slash, and when this second figure is multiplied by the first number, it tells you the length of the gun's barrel. Thus, a 5-inch/54 gun would have an inside barrel diameter of five inches and a barrel length of 270 inches (5 × 54 = 270).

In years past, guns such as the 8-inch/55 and the 16-inch/50 were the main armament of large cruisers and battleships. Today, the most prevalent guns in the U.S. Navy are the 5-inch/54 (on cruisers and destroyers), the 76-mm/62 (on frigates), and a specialized close-in weapons system (CIWS), known as the 20-mm/76 Phalanx system (mounted on many ships as a protection against incoming missile attacks). Many Navy ships also carry saluting guns, which are used for ceremonial purposes and have no combat capability.

Weapon Control Systems

A weapon, however powerful, is only as good as its accuracy. The process by which a projectile, missile, bomb, or torpedo is guided to its target is called weapon control. A potential target is first detected by a sensor (radar, sonar, or lookout). It is then evaluated, either by human judgment or by computer or by a combination of the two. If the target is evaluated to be hostile, a decision is made, according to prescribed weapons doctrine, whether or not to engage. If the target is to be engaged, the appropriate weapon is selected. All available information is assimilated to produce a weapon-control solution that will guide the weapon to contact. The weapon is then fired.

Weapon systems and their components are identified by a "Mark" (abbreviated "Mk") and "Modification" (abbreviated "Mod") system. A new weapon system may be designated the "Mark 22" system, for example. If it were modified later on, the improved system would be called the "Mark 22 Mod 1" system.

Sensors

Before electronics arrived on the scene, enemies were detected and aimed at using the human senses, primarily the eyes. Modern weapons rely on electronic systems for detection of targets and to control weapons. Most common are *radar* and *sonar*. Both operate on the same principle but differ in the medium used.

In its most elemental form, radar (radio detection and ranging) uses a *transceiver* to send out (transmit) a radio-like electronic signal that reflects off a target and then returns the signal to a receiver where a very accurate timing system measures the amount of time that the signal took to travel to and from the target and, using the known speed of the signal, calculates the range to the target. A built-in direction-finding system also provides a bearing (direction) to the target.

Sonar works on the same principle, except that the signal used is *sound* rather than radio waves. Because radio signals work well in air and sound is more effective underwater, radar is used effectively in the detection of surface or air targets, but sonar is the sensor used in the detection of subsurface (underwater) targets.

Radar, sonar, and other Navy electronic equipments are identified by the joint electronics type designation system. This system was originally called the "Army-Navy nomenclature system" and still retains the prefix identifier "AN" (for "Army-Navy"). The rest of the designation consists of three letters plus a number. Each letter tells you something about the equipment, and the number is the series number. For example, referring to Table 14.1, you can see that the designation AN/SPY-1 describes a multifunction (Y) radar (P) that is installed on surface ships (S). It is the first in the series of this type of radar, hence the number 1. If another radar of this type is later developed, it will be the AN/SPY-2.

Systems

Ships, aircraft, and submarines all incorporate various types of weapon-control systems. Surface- and air-search radars have been continuously improved since World War II to detect high-performance targets at long ranges in any weather. The newer surface-ship control systems work with guns and missiles and include radars and digital computers that can quickly acquire and track targets while directing shipboard weapons.

The Mark 86 fire-control system is used in destroyers and larger ships, while the lightweight Mark 92 system is used in missile frigates. The most sophisticated weapon system currently used in U.S. Navy warships is the *Aegis* system, a rapid-reaction, long-range fleet air-defense system capable of effectively handling multiple surface and air targets simultaneously. It includes the very capable AN/SPY-1 radar, a quick-reaction tactical computer for overall command control, a digital weapon-control system, and state-of-the-art guided-missile launchers. Found in *Ticonderoga*-class cruisers and *Arleigh Burke*–class guided missile destroyers, the Aegis system gives a force commander the capability of controlling all of the surface and aerial weapons of an entire battle group in a multi-threat environment.

The SQQ-89 surface-ship antisubmarine warfare (ASW) combat system is an integrated system for detecting, identifying, tracking, and engaging modern submarines.

Submarines and aircraft have their own control systems, similar in general principle to those used in surface ships.

Table 14.1 Joint Electronics Type Designation Systems

Installation		Type of Equipment		Purpose	
A	Airborne	A	Invisible light, heat, radiation	D	Direction finder or reconnaissance
B	Underwater (submarine)	L	Countermeasures	E	Ejection (e.g., chaff)
S	Surface ship	P	Radar	G	Fire Control
U	Multiplatform	Q	Sonar	N	Navigation
W	Surface ship and underwater	R	Radio	Q	Multiple or special purpose
		S	Special	R	Receiving, passive detection
		W	Weapon Related	S	Search
		Y	Data processing	W	Weapon control
				Y	Multifunction

Fleet ballistic missiles fired from submarines are controlled by a missile fire-control system, which is connected to the submarine's inertial navigation system. The navigation system keeps accurate track of the ship's position. When missiles are to be fired, the fire-control system takes current position data and quickly computes firing information to put missiles on the proper ballistic course. While in flight, the missile keeps itself on course with the aid of a built-in navigational system.

Small Arms

The Navy also uses a variety of small arms (pistols, rifles, shotguns, grenade launchers, and machine guns) for various purposes, including sentry duty, riot control, and landing parties.

Just as with larger Navy guns, small arms are differentiated according to the inside diameter (bore) of the barrel. Like larger naval guns, this diameter may be expressed in either inches or millimeters, but unlike larger guns, small arms do not include a follow-on figure representing the length of the barrel (see the previous section). When the figure is in inches, it is referred to as "caliber," as in ".45-caliber pistol," but when it is expressed in millimeters, the term caliber is not used, as in "9-mm pistol."

Shotguns are an exception. They are usually differentiated by "gauge," which still refers to the bore but is defined as the number of lead balls of that particular diameter required to equal a pound. For example, it would take twelve lead balls of the diameter of the 12-gauge shotgun to equal one pound; sixteen balls for the 16-gauge shotgun. This means that the 12-gauge shotgun has a larger bore than the 16-gauge, which seems backwards at first but makes sense when you think about it.

Any weapon with a bore diameter of 0.6 inches (.60-caliber) or less is called a small arm. The largest Navy small arm is the .50-caliber machine gun.

Small arms are considered to be "automatic" if holding down the trigger causes the weapon to continuously fire and "semiautomatic" if the weapon reloads automatically when fired but requires another pull of the trigger to fire off another round.

Some small arms you may encounter are identified by the Army system of terminology. An "M" preceding a number identifies a particular weapon, such as the "M14 rifle." Modifications are identified by a follow-on letter and number combination. For example, the M16 rifle has been modified twice as the M16A1 and M16A2 versions. Sometimes the Navy system of Mk and Mod is used, as in the "20-mm Mk 16 Mod 5 machine gun."

Pistols

One of the oldest weapons in the Navy inventory is the M1911A1 .45-caliber semiautomatic pistol. It is commonly (though erroneously) referred to as the "45-automatic." Because you must pull the trigger each time you fire a round, this pistol is *semiautomatic*. Its magazine holds seven rounds and it has a maximum range of slightly more than 1,600 yards but is usually effective only at about 50 yards. One of its chief advantages is stopping power—where a .38-caliber revolver can be just as lethal as the .45, the latter is more likely to knock a man off his feet, even one who is pumped up on adrenalin. This can be a major asset when dealing with a charging fanatic, for example.

The 9-mm M9 semiautomatic pistol is a similar weapon to the .45-caliber pistol. Slightly lighter in weight, it has a maximum range of 1,962.2 yards (1,800 meters) and an effective range of 54.7 yards (50 meters). A major advantage is that its magazine has a capacity of fifteen rounds, more than double that of the .45 pistol.

The .38-caliber revolver has maximum and effective ranges similar to the .45 pistol, but is lighter in weight. This makes it more suitable for flight personnel. It has a six-round capacity and its relatively simple design makes it unlikely to jam.

The 9-mm pistol is the official replacement for both the .45 and the .38 pistols, but you may find the latter weapons still in service at some commands.

Rifles

As mentioned earlier, you might encounter two versions of the M16 rifle—the M16A1 and the M16A2. Both versions are magazine-fed weapons that fire a 5.56-mm (just slightly larger than a .22-caliber) round. The caliber may seem small, but the high muzzle velocity (more than 3,000 feet per second) makes this a very powerful weapon. The M16A1 has a selector lever that allows the user to fire in automatic or semiautomatic mode, and the M16A2 has a similar selector that permits semiautomatic or burst (three rounds) modes. The magazine capacity is either twenty or thirty rounds, depending upon the type used, and the maximum effective range is 503 yards (460 meters).

While the M16 is the replacement rifle for the Navy, you may still encounter some M14 rifles, capable of firing a 7.62-mm round in either automatic or semiautomatic mode. This was the last of the wooden-stock rifles before lighter plastic ones appeared on the M16. Fully loaded, this rifle weighs in at eleven pounds and has a maximum range of about 4,075 yards.

Shotguns

The most common shotgun in the Navy is the Remington M870. Manually operated, this 12-gauge pump-action shotgun can fire four rounds without reloading. The Mossberg M500 is also a 12-gauge shotgun similar to the M870.

Machine Guns

The .50-caliber M2 Browning machine gun (abbreviated "BMG") is mounted on many surface ships and patrol craft for close-in defense. Ammunition is belt fed at a rate of 450–500 rounds per minute. The BMG has a maximum range of 7,400 yards and an effective range of 2,000 yards. This is a highly effective weapon, but because it is air cooled, there is the danger of a cook-off situation after a burst of 250 rounds or more; you should therefore always keep the weapon laid on target or pointed in a safe direction during breaks in firing. In an extreme case—called runaway firing—the BMG can actually continue firing after the trigger has been released. This can be remedied by twisting the ammunition belt at the feed slot to jam the weapon.

A lighter, but very effective machine gun is the 7.62-mm M60. With a maximum range of 4,075 yards (3,725 meters) and an effective range of 1,200 yards (1,100 meters), the M60 was originally designed for use by ground troops but has been adapted for naval use as well. Firing in short bursts is preferable to continuous firing to prevent overheating.

Grenade Launchers

You may encounter three different kinds of grenade launchers in the Navy. The 40-mm M79 is handheld, like a shotgun, and fires one round (grenade) at a time. The Mk 19 Mod 3 machine gun is a mounted weapon that fires multiple 40-mm grenades in fully automatic bursts. The M203 grenade launcher is actually an accessory that can be attached to the M16A1 rifle.

Major Navy Bases and Air Stations in the United States

15

The following is a list of major naval bases and air stations within the United States. The phone number listed is the main base phone number.

China Lake, California
Commanding Officer
Naval Air Weapons Station
1 Administration Circle
China Lake, CA 93555-6100
(760) 939-9011 • DSN: 437-9011

Lemoore, California
Commanding Officer
Naval Air Station Lemoore
700 Avenger Avenue
Lemoore, CA 93246-5001
(559) 998-3300 • DSN: 949-3300

Monterey, California
Superintendent
Naval Postgraduate School
1 University Circle
Monterey, CA 93943-5001
(831) 656-2441/2 • DSN: 756-2441/2

Point Mugu, California
Commanding Officer
Naval Base Ventura County
Point Magu Naval Air Station
521 9th Street
Point Mugu, CA 93042-5001
(805) 989-1110 • DSN: 351-1110

San Diego, California
Commander, Navy Region Southwest
937 North Harbor Drive
San Diego, CA 92132-5100
Base Information: (619) 556-1011
Surface Ships: (619) 437-2735
Submarines: (619) 553-8643
Aircraft Carrier: To make an appointment please contact the ship directly:
USS *John C. Stennis* (CVN-74) at (619) 545-3647

Commanding Officer
Naval Air Station North Island
P.O. Box 357033
San Diego, CA 92135-7033
Base Information: (619) 545-1011 • DSN: 735-1011

Commanding Officer
Naval Base Coronado
P.O. Box 357033
San Diego, CA 92135-7033
Base Information: (619) 545-1011 • DSN: 735-1011

Commanding Officer
Naval Station San Diego
3455 Senn Road, Room 108
San Diego, CA 92136-5084
Base information: (619) 556-1011 • DSN: 526-1011

Commanding Officer
Naval Submarine Base
140 Sylvester Road
San Diego, CA 92106-3521
Base Information: (619) 553-1011

Commanding Officer
Naval Weapons Station Seal Beach
800 Seal Beach Boulevard
Seal Beach, CA 90740-5000
(562) 626-7000

Groton, Connecticut
Commander
Navy Region Northeast
Box 100
Groton, CT 06349-5100
Base Information: (860) 694-4636 • DSN: 694-4636

Commanding Officer
Naval Submarine Base
Box 100
Groton, CT 06349-5100
Base Information: (860) 694-4636 • DSN: 694-4636

Washington, D.C.
Commandant
Naval District Washington
901 M Street SE
Washington, DC 20374-5001

Commanding Officer
Naval Station Washington
901 M Street SE
Washington, DC 20374-5001

Jacksonville, Florida
Commander, Navy Region Southeast
Box 102, Naval Air Station
Jacksonville, FL 32212-0102
Base Information: (904) 542-2345 • DSN: 942-2345

Commanding Officer
Naval Air Station
Jacksonville, FL 32212-5000
Base Information: (904) 542-2345 • DSN: 942-2345

Commanding Officer
Naval Station
P.O. Box 280112
Mayport, FL 32228-0112
Base Information: (904) 270-5011 • DSN: 960-5011

Key West, Florida
Commanding Officer
Naval Air Station
P.O. Box 9001
804 Sigsbee Road, Building V-4058
Key West, FL 33040-9001
Base Information: (305) 293-4408 ext. 16 • DSN: 483-4408

Pensacola, Florida
Commanding Officer
Naval Air Station Pensacola
190 Radford Boulevard
Pensacola, FL 32508-5217
Base Information: (850) 452-0111 • DSN: 922-0001

Commanding Officer
Naval Air Station Whiting Field
7550 USS Essex Street
Milton, FL 32570-6155
Base Information: (850) 623-7011

Atlanta, Georgia
Commanding Officer
Naval Air Station Atlanta
1000 Halsey Avenue
Marietta, GA 30060-5099
Base Information: (678) 655-1110

Kings Bay, Georgia
Commanding Officer
Naval Submarine Base Kings Bay
1063 USS Tennessee Avenue
Kings Bay, GA 31547-2606
Base Information: (912) 673-2000

Pearl Harbor, Hawaii
Commander
Navy Region, Hawaii
517 Russell Avenue, Suite 110
Pearl Harbor, HI 96860-4884
Base Information: (808) 449-7110 • DSN: 449-7110

Commanding Officer
Naval Station Pearl Harbor
850 Ticonderoga Street, Suite 100
Pearl Harbor, HI 96860-5102

Great Lakes, Illinois
Commander
Naval Training Center
2601A Paul Jones Street
Great Lakes, IL 60088-5000
Base Information: (847) 688-3500

Commanding Officer
Naval Station Great Lakes
Building 1, 2601A Paul Jones Street
Great Lakes, IL 60088
Base Information: (847) 688-3500

Commanding Officer
Recruit Training Command
3301 Indiana Street
Great Lakes, IL 60088-5300
Base Information: (847) 688-3500

New Orleans, Louisiana
Commanding Officer
Naval Air Station Joint Reserve Base New Orleans
400 Russell Avenue
New Orleans, LA 70143-5012
Command Duty Officer: (504) 678-3263/3264 •
DSN: 678-3263/3264

Annapolis, Maryland
Superintendent
United States Naval Academy
121 Blake Road
Annapolis, MD 21402-5000
Base Information: (410) 293-1000 • DSN: 281-1000

Commanding Officer
Naval Station
58 Bennion Road
Annapolis, MD 21402-5054
Base Information: (410) 293-1000 • DSN: 281-1000

Patuxent River, Maryland
Commanding Officer
Naval Air Station
Patuxent River, MD 20670-5409
Base Information: (301) 342-3000 • DSN: 342-3000

Brunswick, Maine
Commanding Officer
Naval Air Station
1251 Orion Street
Brunswick, ME 04011
Base Information: (207) 921-2000

Gulfport, Mississippi
Commanding Officer
Naval Construction Battalion Center
Gulfport, MS
Quarterdeck: (228) 871-2555 • DSN: 868-2555

Meridian, Mississippi
Commanding Officer
Naval Air Station
1155 Rosenbaum Avenue
Meridian, MS 39309-5003
Base Information: (601) 679-2528

Pascagoula, Mississippi
Commanding Officer
Naval Station Pascagoula
Pascagoula, MS 39567-5000
Base Information: (228)761-2140 • DSN: 358-2140

Fallon, Nevada
Commanding Officer
Naval Air Station
Fallon, NV 89406
Base Information: (775) 426-8726 • DSN: 890-8726

Earle, New Jersey
Commanding Officer
Naval Weapons Station Earle
201 Hwy 34 S
Colts Neck, NJ 07722-5001
Base Information: (732) 866-2500

Willow Grove, Pennsylvania
Commanding Officer
Naval Air Station Willow Grove
P.O. Box 21
Willow Grove, PA 19090-5021
Public Affairs Office: (215) 443-1776

Newport, Rhode Island
Commanding Officer
Naval Station Newport
690 Peary Street
Newport, RI 02841-1522
Base Information: (401) 841-3456

Charleston, South Carolina
Commanding Officer
Naval Weapons Station Charleston
2316 Red Bank Road
Goose Greek, SC 29445-8601
Base Information: (843) 764-7000

Millington, Tennessee
Commanding Officer
Naval Support Activity Mid-South
7800 Integrity Avenue
Millington, TN 38054
Base Information: (901) 874-5509

Corpus Christi, Texas
Commanding Officer
Naval Air Station Corpus Christi
11001 D Street, Suite 143
Corpus Christi, TX 78419-5021
Base Information: (361) 961-2811

Fort Worth, Texas
Commanding Officer
Naval Air Station Ft. Worth
11001 D Street, Suite 143
Ft. Worth, TX 78419-5021
Base Information: (817) 782-7152

Ingleside, Texas
Commanding Officer
Naval Station Ingleside
1455 Ticonderoga Road
Ingleside, TX 78362-5001
Base Information: (361) 776-5781 • DSN: 776-5781

Kingsville, Texas
Commanding Officer
Naval Air Station Kingsville
554 McCain Street
Kingsville, TX 78363-5053
Base Information: (361) 516-6333 • DSN: 876-6333

Norfolk, Virginia
Commander
Navy Region Mid-Atlantic
6506 Hampton Boulevard
Norfolk, VA 23508-1273
Base Information: (757) 444-0000 • DSN: 564-0000 Ships

Tour and Information Office
9079 Hampton Boulevard
Norfolk, VA 23505-1092
(757) 444-7955

Commanding Officer
Naval Station
1653 Morris Street
Norfolk, VA 23511-2895
Base Information: (757) 444-0000

Commanding Officer
Naval Amphibious Base Little Creek
2600 Tarawa Court
Norfolk, VA 23521-3297
Base Information: (757) 444-0000 • DSN: 564-0111

Commanding Officer
Naval Air Station Oceana
Virginia Beach, VA 23460-5120
Base Information: (757) 444-0000 • DSN: 564-0111

Bangor, Washington
Commander
Navy Region Northwest
1103 Hunley Road
Silverdale, WA 98315-1199
Base Information: (360) 396-6111 • DSN: 744-6111

Commander
Naval Submarine Base Bangor
1100 Hunley Road
Silverdale, WA 98315-1199
Base Information: (360) 396-6111 • DSN: 744-6111

Bremerton, Washington
Commanding Officer
Naval Station Bremerton
120 South Dewey
Bremerton, WA 98314-5020
Base Information: (360) 476-3711 • DSN: 439-3711

Everett, Washington
Commanding Officer
Naval Station Everett
2000 West Marine View
Everett, WA 98207-5001
Base Information: (425) 304-3000 • DSN: 727-3000

Whidbey Island, Washington
Commanding Officer
Naval Air Station Whidbey Island
3730 North Charles Porter Avenue
Oak Harbor, WA 98278-5000
Base Information: (360) 257-2211 • DSN: 820-2211

Ranks, Rates, and Ratings   16

Enlisted Rates

The use of the word *rank* for Navy enlisted personnel is incorrect. The term is *rate*. The rating badge is a combination of rate (pay grade, as indicated by the chevrons) and rating (occupational specialty, as indicated by the symbol just above the chevrons).

A rating badge is worn on the upper left sleeve of all uniforms in grades E-4 through E-6. Chief petty officers (E-7 through E-9) wear collar devices on their white and khaki uniforms and rating badges on their service dress blues.

The enlisted rating badge for Petty Officer Third Class and higher consists of two parts. The chevrons indicate pay grade (rate). Between the chevrons and the eagle is an insignia indicating the sailor's job specialty (rating). Insignia are white on blue uniforms and navy blue on white uniforms. Sailors in pay grades E-4 through E-6 can be addressed as "Petty Officer (surname)" or "Boatswain's Mate Third Class (surname)," for example. Chief petty officers are always referred to as "Chief," "Senior Chief," or "Master Chief," as appropriate.

Enlisted Rate Insignia

The rating badge—a combination of rate (pay grade) and rating (specialty)—is worn on the upper left sleeve of all uniforms in grades E-4 through E-6. E-1 through E-3 wear color-coded group rate marks based upon their occupational field. Group rate marks for E-1 (optional) through E-3 are worn on dress uniforms only. Chief petty officers (E-7 through E-9) wear collar devices on their white and khaki uniforms and rate badges on their service dress blues. Enlisted rate insignia are presented in appendix B.

Ratings—Administration, Deck, Medical, Technical, and Weapons Specialties

Following are the rating insignia for administration, deck, medical, and weapons specialties:

BM

Crossed anchors

CT

Crossed quill and spark

DK

Key on data card

DM

Draftsman's compass on triangle

DT

"D" on caduceus

ET

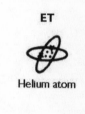

Helium atom

EW

Spark through helium atom

FC

Range finder with inward spark on each side

FT

Range finder

GM

Crossed cannons

HM

Caduceus

IS

Magnifying glass
and quill

IT

Four sparks

JO

Crossed quill
and scroll

LI

Crossed lith crayon
holder and scraper

LN

Vertical millrind
crossing quill

MA

Star embossed in
circle within shield

MN

Floating mine

MT

Guided missile and
electronic wave

MU

Lyre

NC

Anchor crossed
with quill

OS

Arrow through
oscilloscope

PC

Postal cancellation
mark

PN

Crossed manual
and quill

QM

Ship's helm

RP

Globe on anchor
within compass

SH

Crossed key
and quill

SK

Crossed keys

SM

Crossed semaphore
flags

ST

Earphones pierced
by arrow

TM

Torpedo

YN

Crossed quills

Note 1: As this book goes to press, "Cryptologic Technician" consists of six branches: CTA (Cryptologic Technician—Administration); CTI (Cryptologic Technician—Interpretive); CTM (Cryptologic Technician—Maintenance); CTO (Cryptologic Technician—Communications); CTR (Cryptologic Technician—Collection); and CTT (Cryptologic Technician—Technical). However, the Navy plans to retire CTM and CTO and add CTN (Cryptologic Technician—Networks).

Note 2: As this book goes to press, the Navy plans to fold DK into PN and rename it PS: Personnel Specialist. The PN rating badge would be retained.

Note 3: "Gunner's Mate" is used at pay grade E-7 and higher. Leading to GM: GMG (Gunner's Mate—Guns) and GMM (Gunner's Mate—Missiles)

Note 4: Formerly known as RM (Radioman). DP (Data Processing Technician) merged into the IT (Information Systems Technician) field on 4 November 1999.

Note 5: "Sonar Technician" has two branches: STG—Surface and STS—Submarine.

Ratings—Engineering and Hull Specialties

Following are the rating insignia for engineering and hull specialties.

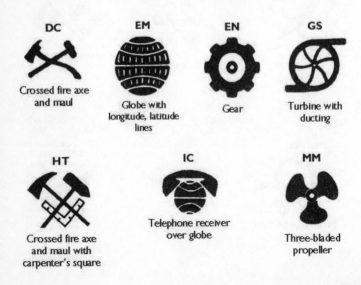

DC
Crossed fire axe
and maul

EM
Globe with
longitude, latitude
lines

EN
Gear

GS
Turbine with
ducting

HT
Crossed fire axe
and maul with
carpenter's square

IC
Telephone receiver
over globe

MM
Three-bladed
propeller

Note: "Gas Turbine System Technician" is used at pay grade E-9 only. Leading to GS: GSE (Gas Turbine System Technician—Electrical) and GSM (Gas Turbine System Technician—Mechanical).

Rating—Aviation Specialties

Following are the rating insignia for aviation specialties:

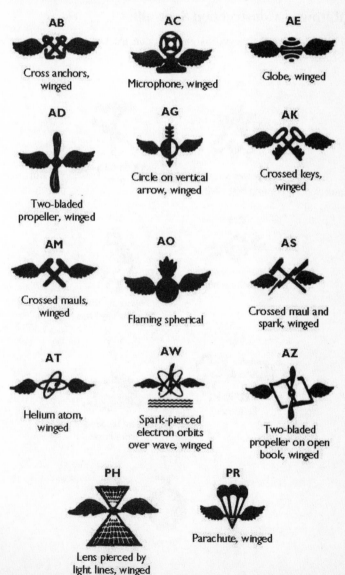

AB
Cross anchors, winged

AC
Microphone, winged

AE
Globe, winged

AD
Two-bladed propeller, winged

AG
Circle on vertical arrow, winged

AK
Crossed keys, winged

AM
Crossed mauls, winged

AO
Flaming spherical

AS
Crossed maul and spark, winged

AT
Helium atom, winged

AW
Spark-pierced electron orbits over wave, winged

AZ
Two-bladed propeller on open book, winged

PH
Lens pierced by light lines, winged

PR
Parachute, winged

Note 1: "Aviation Boatswain's Mate" is used at pay grade E-9 only. Leading to AB: ABE (Launching and Recovery of Aircraft), ABF (Fuels and ABH, which is Aircraft Handling).

Note 2: "Aviation Structural Mechanic" is used at pay grade E-8 only. Leading to AM: AME (Safety Equipment), AMH (Hydraulics), and AMS (Structures).

Ratings—Construction Specialties

Following are the rating insignia for construction specialties (the Seabees):

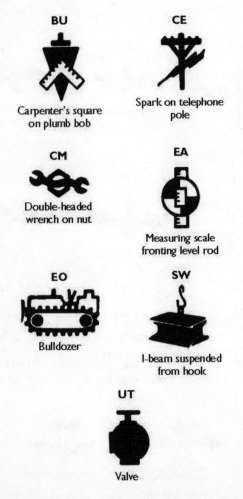

BU — Carpenter's square on plumb bob

CE — Spark on telephone pole

CM — Double-headed wrench on nut

EA — Measuring scale fronting level rod

EO — Bulldozer

SW — I-beam suspended from hook

UT — Valve

Note 1: BU, EA, and SW become CUCM at pay grade E-9.
Note 2: CE and UT become UCCM at pay grade E-9.
Note 3: CM and EO become EQCM at pay grade E-9.

Officer Ranks

Navy officers wear their rank devices in different places on their uniforms, depending upon the uniform. The three basic uniforms and the type of rank devices are khakis (a working uniform) with pins on the collar, whites with stripes on shoulder boards, and blues with stripes sewn on the lower sleeve. Shoulder boards are also worn on bridge coats and reefers. The collar devices are also worn on the right side of the garrison cap (a miniature officer's crest is worn on the left), and slightly larger devices are worn on the epaulets of the raincoat and working jacket.

Additionally, line officers wear a star above the stripes of the shoulder boards or sleeves but staff and warrant officers wear specialty insignia. Officer insignia are presented in the appendix.

Specialty Insignia

Officers in the Navy are either line officers or staff corps. Among these are also limited duty officers and commissioned warrant officers. Staff corps and commissioned warrant officers wear insignia in place of the line officer's star. The following sections describe the specialty insignia of the staff corps and LDO and warrant officers.

Specialty Insignia—Staff Corps Officers

Commissioned officers of the staff corps are specialists in career fields that are professions unto themselves, such as physicians, lawyers, civil engineers, and so on. Staff corps officers wear their specialty insignia on the sleeves of the dress blue uniforms and on their shoulder boards in place of the star worn by line officers. On winter blue and khaki uniforms, the specialty insignia is a collar device worn on the left collar, while the rank device is worn on the right.

Specialty Insignia—LDO and Warrant Officers

Some commissioned officers have advanced through the enlisted rates and are designated for duty in certain technical fields. These are limited duty officers (LDO) and commissioned warrant offi-

cers (CWO). Staff corps LDOs and CWOs wear their specialty insignia on the sleeves of the dress blue uniforms and on their shoulder boards in place of the star worn by line officers. On winter
blue and khaki uniforms, the specialty insignia is a collar device
worn on the left collar, while the rank device is worn on the right.

Warfare and Other Qualifications

Navy personnel who have achieved certain professional warfare
and other qualifications may wear one or two (if more than one
has been earned) identifying emblems, or pins, on their left breast.
The exception is the command pin worn on the right breast when
in command and on the left breast when no longer in command.

Correspondence Forms of Address

17

YN2 Sam D. Sluka III, USN

The following examples of military models of address, salutation, and complimentary close are used in the preparation of Navy business-format letters. They may be varied depending on circumstances. Reference: Secretary of the Navy Instruction 5216.5: Navy Correspondence Manual.

Navy and Coast Guard Officers

Addressee	Letter and Envelope	Salutation
Admiral	ADM	Dear Admiral (surname):
Vice Admiral	VADM	Dear Admiral (surname):
Rear Admiral (Upper Half)	RADM	Dear Admiral (surname):
Rear Admiral (Lower Half)	RDML	Dear Admiral (surname):
Captain	CAPT	Dear Captain (surname):
Commander	CDR	Dear Commander (surname):
Lieutenant Commander	LCDR	Dear Commander (surname):
Lieutenant	LT	Dear Lieutenant (surname):
Lieutenant Junior Grade	LTJG	Dear Lieutenant (surname):
Ensign	ENS	Dear Ensign (surname):
Chief Warrant Officer	CWO5	Dear Chief Warrant Officer (surname):
	CWO4	Dear Chief Warrant Officer (surname):
	CWO3	Dear Chief Warrant Officer (surname):
	CWO2	Dear Chief Warrant Officer (surname):

Marine Corps, Air Force, and Army Officers

	Marines	Air Force	Army	Salutation
General	Gen	Gen	GEN	Dear General (surname):
Lieutenant General	LtGen	Lt Gen	LTG	Dear General (surname):
Major General	MajGen	Maj Gen	MG	Dear General (surname):
Brigadier General	BGen	Brig Gen	BG	Dear General (surname):
Colonel	Col	Col	COL	Dear Colonel (surname):
Lieutenant Colonel	LtCol	Lt Col	LTC	Dear Colonel (surname):
Major	Maj	Maj	Maj	Dear Major (surname):
Captain	Capt	Capt	Capt	Dear Captain (surname):
First Lieutenant	1stLt	1st Lt	1LT	Dear Lieutenant (surname):
Second Lieutenant	2ndLt	2nd Lt	2LT	Dear Lieutenant (surname):
Chief Warrant Officer 5	CWO5	CW5	Dear Chief Warrant Officer (surname):	
Chief Warrant Officer 4	CWO4	CW4	Dear Chief Warrant Officer (surname):	
Chief Warrant Officer 3	CWO3	CW3	Dear Chief Warrant Officer (surname):	
Chief Warrant Officer 2	CWO2	CW2	Dear Chief Warrant Officer (surname):	
Warrant Officer	WO	WO1	Dear Warrant Officer (surname):	

Navy and Coast Guard Enlisted

Addressee	Letter and Envelope	Salutation
Master Chief Petty Officer of the Navy	MCPON	Dear Master Chief (surname):
Master Chief Petty Officer of the Coast Guard	MCPOCG	Dear Master Chief (surname):
Master Chief Petty Officer	MCPO	Dear Master Chief (surname):
Senior Chief Petty Officer	SCPO	Dear Senior Chief (surname):
Chief Petty Officer	CPO	Dear Chief (surname):
Petty Officer First Class	PO1	Dear Petty Officer (surname):
Petty Officer Second Class	PO2	Dear Petty Officer (surname):
Petty Officer Third Class	PO3	Dear Petty Officer (surname):
Airman (includes Apprentice and Recruit)	AN or AA or AR	Dear Airman (surname):
Constructionman (includes Apprentice and Recruit)	CN or CA or CR	Dear Constructionman (surname):
Dentalman (includes Apprentice and Recruit)	DN or DA or DR	Dear Dentalman (surname):
Fireman (includes Apprentice and Recruit)	FN or FA or FR	Dear Fireman (surname):
Hospitalman (includes Apprentice and Recruit)	HN or HA or HR	Dear Hospitalman (surname):
Seaman (includes Apprentice and Recruit)	SN or SA or SR	Dear Seaman (surname):

Marine Corps Enlisted

Addressee	Letter and Envelope	Salutation
Sergeant Major of the Marine Corps	SgtMaj	Dear Sergeant Major (surname):
Sergeant Major	SgtMaj	Dear Sergeant Major (surname):
Master Gunnery Sergeant	MgySgt	Dear Master Gunnery Sergeant (surname):
First Sergeant	1stSgt	Dear First Sergeant (surname):
Master Sergeant	MSgt	Dear Master Sergeant (surname):
Gunnery Sergeant	GySgt	Dear Gunnery Sergeant (surname):
Staff Sergeant	SSgt	Dear Staff Sergeant (surname):
Sergeant	Sgt	Dear Sergeant (surname):
Corporal	Cpl	Dear Corporal (surname):
Lance Corporal	LCpl	Dear Corporal (surname):
Private First Class	PFC	Dear Private First Class (surname):
Private	Pvt	Dear Private (surname):

Army Enlisted

Addressee	Letter and Envelope	Salutation
Sergeant Major of the Army	SMA	Dear Sergeant Major (surname):
Command Sergeant Major	CSM	Dear Sergeant Major (surname):
Sergeant Major	SGM	Dear Sergeant Major (surname):
First Sergeant	1SG	Dear First Sergeant (surname):
Master Sergeant	MSG	Dear Master Sergeant (surname):
Platoon Sergeant	PSG	Dear Sergeant (surname):
Sergeant First Class	SFC	Dear Sergeant (surname):
Staff Sergeant	SSG	Dear Sergeant (surname):
Sergeant	SGT	Dear Sergeant (surname):
Corporal	CPL	Dear Corporal (surname):
Private First Class	PFC	Dear Private (surname):
Private	PVT	Dear Private (surname):
Specialists (all grades)	SP7	Dear Specialist (surname):
	SP6	Dear Specialist (surname):
	(Etc)	Dear Specialist (surname):

Air Force Enlisted

Addressee	Letter and Envelope	Salutation
Chief Master Sergeant of the Air Force	CMSAF	Dear Chief (surname):
Chief Master Sergeant	CMSgt	Dear Chief (surname):
Senior Master Sergeant	SMSgt	Dear Sergeant (surname):
Master Sergeant	MSgt	Dear Sergeant (surname):
Technical Sergeant	TSgt	Dear Sergeant (surname):
Staff Sergeant	SSgt	Dear Sergeant (surname):
Sergeant	Sgt	Dear Sergeant (surname):
Senior Airman	SrA	Dear Airman (surname):
Airman First Class	A1C	Dear Airman (surname):
Airman	Amn	Dear Airman (surname):
Airman Basic	AB	Dear Airman (surname):

Other Military

Addressee	Letter and Envelope	Salutation
All retired military	(Rank) (full name), (USN, USMCR, or other branch) (Ret)	Dear (rank) (surname):
Chaplain	(Rank) (full name) CHC, USN	Dear Chaplain (surname):

Military Time

18

Time is told on a continuous twenty-four-hour clock. Rather than distinguishing between morning (AM) and afternoon (PM), the time is read sequentially from 0001 to 2400.

Fifteen minutes past midnight is written as 0015 and spoken as "zero, zero, fifteen."

One thirty in the morning is written as 0130 and spoken as "zero, one, thirty."

Two o'clock in the afternoon is two hours after twelve and therefore is written as 1400 and spoken as "fourteen hundred."

Quarter to ten in the evening is written as 2145 and spoken as "twenty-one, forty-five."

After midnight, one o'clock is spoken as "zero, one hundred." After noon, it is spoken as "thirteen hundred."

In the morning, five o'clock is spoken as "zero, five hundred." In the afternoon, it is "seventeen hundred."

Before noon, ten o'clock is "ten hundred." At night, it is referred to as "twenty-two hundred."

Useful Naval Web Sites   19

The following is a list of useful Web sites related to the U.S. Navy and Marine Corps. While this list of Web sites was checked for accuracy shortly before the manuscript went into production, Web sites come and go, and sometimes they move! If a Web site listed here is no longer available, it is recommended that you use a Web search engine, such as http://www.google.com, to search for the related topic.

The U.S. Navy

Web Site for Official Information About the U.S. Navy
http://www.navy.mil/

A

Academy, United States Naval
http://www.usna.edu/
Acquisition and Business Management, Navy
http://www.abm.rda.hq.navy.mil/
Acquisition Reform, Navy
http://www.acq-ref.navy.mil/index.cfm
Advancement Results from the Navy Personnel Command Web Site
http://www.bupers.navy.mil/selectbd/index.html
Aircraft
http://www.chinfo.navy.mil/navpalib/factfile/ffiletop.html
Aircraft Carriers
http://www.chinfo.navy.mil/navpalib/ships/carriers/
Aircraft Carriers—Navy Fact File Page
http://www.chinfo.navy.mil/navpalib/factfile/ships/ship-cv.html
Aircraft Carrier—A Brief Illustrated History: The Early Years
http://www.chinfo.navy.mil/navpalib/ships/carriers/cv-hist1.html

Aircraft Carrier—A Brief Illustrated History: The Escort ("Jeep") Carriers
http://www.chinfo.navy.mil/navpalib/ships/carriers/cv-escrt.html

Aircraft Carrier—A Brief Illustrated History: Korea and the 1950s
http://www.chinfo.navy.mil/navpalib/ships/carriers/cv-hist4.html

Aircraft Carrier—A Brief Illustrated History: Post World War II
http://www.chinfo.navy.mil/navpalib/ships/carriers/cv-hist3.html

Aircraft Carrier—A Brief Illustrated History: Space and Vietnam
http://www.chinfo.navy.mil/navpalib/ships/carriers/partv/cv-hist5.html

Aircraft Carrier—A Brief Illustrated History: World War II—1941–1942
http://www.chinfo.navy.mil/navpalib/ships/carriers/cv-hist2.html

Aircraft Carrier—A Brief Illustrated History: World War II—1943
http://www.chinfo.navy.mil/navpalib/ships/carriers/cv-hist2b.html

Aircraft Carrier—A Brief Illustrated History: World War II—1944–1945
http://www.chinfo.navy.mil/navpalib/ships/carriers/cv-hist2c.html

Aircraft Carriers—Digital Images
http://www.chinfo.navy.mil/navpalib/images/image-cv.html

Aircraft Carriers—List of
http://www.chinfo.navy.mil/navpalib/ships/carriers/cv-list1.html

Air Force Link—The Web Site of the U.S. Air Force
http://www.af.mil/

Air Shows (Aviation Events)
http://www.chinfo.navy.mil/navpalib/aircraft/airshows/airshows.html

Air Stations and Bases—Naval
http://www.chinfo.navy.mil/navpalib/bases/navbases.html

All Hands—The Magazine of the U.S. Navy
http://www.news.navy.mil/allhands.asp

American Flag—How to Display
   http://www.chinfo.navy.mil/navpalib/allhands/ah0697/jun-
   pg18.html
American Forces Information Service (AFIS)
   http://www.defenselink.mil/afis/
American Red Cross
   http://www.redcross.org/
Anchor Desk—A Gateway to Navy support
   http://www.anchordesk.navy.mil/index.htm
Anchors Aweigh
   http://www.chinfo.navy.mil/navpalib/traditions/music/
   anchor1.html
Anthrax Information
   http://www.chinfo.navy.mil/navpalib/anthrax/anthrax.html
Anthrax Vaccination Program for the Military
   http://www.anthrax.mil/
Arizona Memorial, Pearl Harbor, Hawaii
   http://www.nps.gov/usar/index.htm
ArmyLink—The Web Site of the U.S. Army
   http://www.army.mil/
Assistant Secretary of the Navy, Financial Management and
   Comptroller
   http://navweb.secnav.navy.mil/
Assistant Secretary of the Navy, Installation and Environment
   http://www.chinfo.navy.mil/navpalib/people/assistsecnav/
   asn_ie/asn_ie.html
Assistant Secretary of the Navy, Manpower, and Reserve Affairs
   http://www.chinfo.navy.mil/navpalib/people/assistsecnav/
   asn_mra/asn_mra.html
Assistant Secretary of the Navy, Research, Development, and
   Acquisition
   http://www.hq.navy.mil/RDA/
Aviation, National Museum of Naval
   http://www.naval-air.org/
Aviation News, Naval—The Magazine of U.S. Navy Aviation
   http://history.navy.mil/branches/nhcorg5.htm
Aviation Ordnance Officers Career Progression (AOOCP)
   Training
   https://www.cnet.navy.mil/nascweb/aoocp/aoos.htm

B

Bachelor Quarters—Navy Bachelor Housing Office
http://www.navfac.navy.mil/housing/index.htm

Badges—Breast Insignia and Badges
http://www.chinfo.navy.mil/navpalib/ranks/officers/breast-insignia/insignia.html

Band Schedules, History, etc., of the U.S. Navy Band, Washington, D.C.
http://www.navyband.navy.mil/

Bands—Links to Various Navy Bands
http://www.bupers.navy.mil/navymusic/bands.htm

Battleships
http://www.chinfo.navy.mil/navpalib/ships/battleships/

Battleships in the U.S. Navy, A Brief History of
http://www.chinfo.navy.mil/navpalib/ships/battleships/bbhistory.html

Battleships, A List of All Former U.S. Navy
http://www.chinfo.navy.mil/navpalib/ships/battleships/bb-list1.html

Battleship List, Naval Vessel Register
http://www.nvr.navy.mil/nvrships/S_bb.htm

Biographies of Navy Leadership
http://www.chinfo.navy.mil/navpalib/people/flags/biographies/bios-top.html

Blue Angels—U.S. Navy Flight Demonstration Squadron—Web Site with the Current Schedule
http://www.navy.com/jsp/explore/comunity/blueangels/index.jsp?cid=28&pid=2&flashEnabled=false

Breast Insignia and Badges
http://www.chinfo.navy.mil/navpalib/ranks/officers/breast-insignia/insignia.html

Budget, Navy—FY2005
http://navweb.secnav.navy.mil/pubbud/05pres/db_u.htm

Burial at Sea
http://www.chinfo.navy.mil/navpalib/questions/burial.html

Business, Doing, with the Military—From the Department of Defense Web Site
http://www.defenselink.mil/other_info/business.html

C

Captain's Call Kit
  http://www.news.navy.mil/search/ccklist.asp
Career Development, Navy Personnel Command's Center for
  http://www.staynavy.navy.mil/
Centennial of the Submarine in the U.S. Navy
  http://www.chinfo.navy.mil/navpalib/ships/submarines/
  sub100.html
Ceremonial Music, Marches, and Selected Music, Performed
  by the U.S. Navy Band
  http://www.bupers.navy.mil/navymusic/audio.htm
Chaplains, Chief of
  http://www.chaplain.navy.mil/
Chief Information Officer, Department of the Navy—Information Technology
  http://www.doncio.navy.mil/(dpssp5fhw0igm145srnuq055)/
  main.aspx
ChaplainCare
  http://www.chaplaincare.navy.mil/index.htm
Chief Petty Officers—Remarks by CNO, 8 November 1994
  http://www.chinfo.navy.mil/navpalib/people/chiefs/
  boor1105.txt
Chiefs of Naval Operations
  http://www.chinfo.navy.mil/navpalib/people/cno/cno-list.
  html
Child Care
  http://mfrc.calib.com/mcy/
Chips—The Navy's Technical Journal
  http://www.chips.navy.mil/
Civil War Sailors Database—From the National Park Service
  http://www.itd.nps.gov/cwss/sailors_index.html
Civil Engineer, Navy—Magazine of the Civil Engineering
  Corps. (CEC)
  http://www.navfac.navy.mil/nce/
CNET Programs
  https://www.cnet.navy.mil/programs.html
Coast Guard—The Web Site of the U.S. Coast Guard. The
  Coast Guard is an agency of the Department of Homeland
  Security and reports to the Navy during times of war.
  http://www.uscg.mil/USCG.shtm

D

Dictionary of Military Terms
   http://www.dtic.mil/doctrine/jel/new_pubs/jp1_02.pdf
DD(X)
   http://peoships.crane.navy.mil/ddx/
Detailers—Officer and Enlisted
   http://www.persnet.navy.mil/pers4/index.html
Digital Imagery of the U.S. Navy
   http://www.news.navy.mil/view_featured.asp
Direct Commission Officer School
   https://www.cnet.navy.mil/nascweb/dco/dco.htm
Directives—Navy (Instructions and Notices)
   http://neds.nebt.daps.mil/
DirectLine—The Newsletter from the Master Chief Petty Officer of the Navy
   http://www.persnet.navy.mil/mcpon/directline/
Distance Support—Anchor Desk, a Navy Support Web Site
   http://www.anchordesk.navy.mil/index.htm
Dolphins—The Navy's Marine Mammal Program
   http://www.spawar.navy.mil/sandiego/technology/
   mammals/

E

Emergency Communication or Notification of Service Members, by the American Red Cross
   http://www.redcross.org/services/afes/0,1082,0_476_,00.
   html
Emergency Services, Armed Forces—From the American Red
   Cross
   http://www.redcross.org/services/afes/0,1082,0_321_,00.
   html
Employment Opportunities with the Federal Government, Including the Department of the Navy—Fed World
   http://www.fedworld.gov/jobs/jobsearch.html
Environment—Department of the Navy Environmental Program
   http://web.dandp.com/enviroweb/index.html
Eternal Father ("Navy Hymn")
   http://www.chinfo.navy.mil/navpalib/questions/eternal.html
Europe—Commander, U.S. Naval Forces
   http://www.naveur.navy.mil/

EXCEL, Task Force—CNO's Initiative to Revolutionize Navy
Training
http://www.excel.navy.mil/
Exchange, Navy—Navy Exchange Command
http://www.navy-nex.com/

F

F/A-18, Fact File Page on
http://www.chinfo.navy.mil/navpalib/factfile/aircraft/air-
fa18.html
F/A-18E/F Super Hornet
http://www.chinfo.navy.mil/navpalib/aircraft/fa18/shor-
net.html
F/A-18E/F Super Hornet Weapons Load Out
http://www.chinfo.navy.mil/navpalib/aircraft/fa18/fa18ord.
html
Fact File—Facts Sheets on Aircraft, Ships, Personnel, etc.
http://www.chinfo.navy.mil/navpalib/factfile/ffiletop.html
Family Assistance—From DoD's Web Site
http://dod.mil/mapsite/
FirstGov—U.S. Government Web Portal
http://firstgov.gov/
Fitness—Physical Readiness Program, Navy
http://www.mwr.navy.mil/mwrprgms/physred.htm
Flag, How to Display the United States
http://www.chinfo.navy.mil/navpalib/allhands/ah0697/jun-
pg18.html
Flag Officer Biographies
http://www.chinfo.navy.mil/navpalib/people/flags/
biographies/bios-top.html
Fleet Home Town News Center—A Field Activity of the Navy
Office of Information
http://www.chinfo.navy.mil/navpalib/chinfo/fhtnc.html
Fleet, Commander, Fifth
http://www.cusnc.navy.mil/
Fleet, Commander, Second
http://www.secondflt.navy.mil/
Fleet, Commander, Seventh
http://www.c7f.navy.mil/

Fleet, Commander, Third (and USS *Coronado*)
http://www.comthirdflt.navy.mil/

Fleet, Commander, U.S. Atlantic
http://www.atlanticfleet.navy.mil/

Fleet, Commander, U.S. Pacific
http://www.cpf.navy.mil/

Forms—Department of Defense
http://web1.whs.osd.mil/icdhome/forms.htm

Forms—Department of the Navy
http://neds.nebt.daps.mil/Directives/navyform.htm

Forms—Various U.S. Government Agencies
http://www.fedforms.gov/

Forward Presence—Written by the Chief of Naval Operations
and the Commandant of the Marine Corps December 1996
http://www.chinfo.navy.mil/navpalib/policy/fromsea/fwd-
presn.html

Freedom of Information Online Resource Center—Department
of the Navy's Freedom of Information Act Program.
http://foia.navy.mil/

Frequently Asked Questions About the Navy
http://www.chinfo.navy.mil/navpalib/.www/faq.html

" . . . From the Sea" (9/92)
http://www.chinfo.navy.mil/navpalib/policy/fromsea/from-
sea.txt

"Forward . . . From the Sea" (11/94), Update to the Original
Document
http://www.chinfo.navy.mil/navpalib/policy/fromsea/
forward.txt

"Forward . . . From the Sea," The Navy Operational Concept
(3/97)
http://www.chinfo.navy.mil/navpalib/policy/fromsea/
ffseanoc.html

" . . . From the Sea" Update: Carriers for Force 2001 (5/93)
http://www.chinfo.navy.mil/navpalib/policy/fromsea/
ftsucf2.txt

" . . . From the Sea" Update: Force Sustainment (5/93)
http://www.chinfo.navy.mil/navpalib/policy/fromsea/
ftsufs.txt

" . . . From the Sea" Update: Joint Operations (5/93)
http://www.chinfo.navy.mil/navpalib/policy/fromsea/
ftsujo.txt

" . . . From the Sea" Update: Naval Forward Presence: Essential
for a Changing World (5/93)
http://www.chinfo.navy.mil/navpalib/policy/fromsea/
ftsunfp.txt

" . . . From the Sea" Update: The OpNav Assessment Process
(5/93)
http://www.chinfo.navy.mil/navpalib/policy/fromsea/
ftsuoap.txt

Funeral Honors, Requesting
http://www.chinfo.navy.mil/navpalib/questions/
burial2.html

G

General Counsel of the Department of the Navy
http://www.chinfo.navy.mil/navpalib/people/gencounsel/
morabio.html

General Counsel, Office of the
http://www.ogc.navy.mil/

Government, U.S., Web Portal—FirstGov
http://firstgov.gov/

GulfLINK—The Official Source for Information on Gulf War
Illnesses
http://www.gulflink.osd.mil/

H

Historical Center, Naval, Washington, D.C.
http://www.history.navy.mil/

Holiday Messages—Armed Forces Day
http://www.chinfo.navy.mil/navpalib/holidays/armdfrcs/

Holiday Messages—Christmas
http://www.chinfo.navy.mil/navpalib/holidays/xmas/

Holiday Messages—Directory List
http://www.chinfo.navy.mil/navpalib/holidays/

Holiday Messages—Independence Day
http://www.chinfo.navy.mil/navpalib/holidays/july4/

Holiday Messages—Martin Luther King, Jr.
http://www.chinfo.navy.mil/navpalib/holidays/mlking/

Holiday Messages—Memorial Day
http://www.chinfo.navy.mil/navpalib/holidays/memorial/

Holiday Messages—Navy Birthday
http://www.chinfo.navy.mil/navpalib/holidays/navybday/
Holiday Messages—POW-MIA Day
http://www.chinfo.navy.mil/navpalib/holidays/powmia/
Holiday Messages—Thanksgiving
http://www.chinfo.navy.mil/navpalib/holidays/thanksgv/
Holiday Messages—Veterans Day
http://www.chinfo.navy.mil/navpalib/holidays/vetsday/
Homeland Security, Department of
http://www.dhs.gov/dhspublic/
Homeport List—Alphabetical List of Navy's Home Ports and
the Ships Assigned
http://www.chinfo.navy.mil/navpalib/ships/lists/
homeport.html
Household Goods—Moving
http://207.132.136.34/navsuphhg/index.htm
Housing Homepage, Navy
http://www.housing.navy.mil/
Human Resources Office, Navy Secretariat/Headquarters—
Employment opportunities with the U.S. Navy in the Washington, D.C., Area
http://www.hq.navy.mil/shhro/
Human Resources Online, Department of the Navy Deputy Assistant Secretary of the Navy for Civilian Personnel and Equal
Employment Opportunity [DASN (CP/EEO)] and the Department of the Navy Human Resources Operations Center
(HROC): DoN civilian vacancy and training announcements
and other information
http://www.donhr.navy.mil/
Hymn, Navy (Eternal Father)
http://www.chinfo.navy.mil/navpalib/questions/eternal.html

I

Images of the Navy
http://www.news.navy.mil/view_featured.asp
Information Offices, Navy—Field Offices of the Chief of Information
http://www.chinfo.navy.mil/navpalib/chinfo/fldacts.html
Insignia—Breast Insignia and Badges
http://www.chinfo.navy.mil/navpalib/ranks/officers/breast-
insignia/insignia.html

Intranet, Navy-Marine Corps
  http://www.nmci.navy.mil/
Inventory Control Point, Naval
  http://www.navicp.navy.mil/
ITempo [Individual Personnel Tempo]—From the Navy Personnel Command Web Site
  http://www.bupers.navy.mil/itempo/itempo.htm

J

JAGMAN Handbook—How to Conduct JAG Manual Investigations (Zipped WordPerfect)
  http://www.chinfo.navy.mil/navpalib/policy/jagman.zip
Jones, John Paul
  http://www.chinfo.navy.mil/navpalib/traditions/html/jpjones.html
Judge Advocate General's Corps
  http://www.jag.navy.mil/index.htm
Junior Reserve Officer Training Corps, Naval (NJROTC)
  https://www.njrotc.navy.mil/

K

Knowledge Online, Navy
  https://wwwa.nko.navy.mil/
Korean War—50th Anniversary Commemorative Site
  http://korea50.army.mil/

L

LDO/CWO Indoctrination School
  https://www.cnet.navy.mil/nascweb/mustang/mustang.htm
LDO/CWO Page from NAVPERS Site
  http://www.bupers.navy.mil/pers211/index.html
Leadership Continuum, The
  https://www.cnet.navy.mil/leadcon.html
Leadership, Navy
  http://www.chinfo.navy.mil/navpalib/people/leadership/leadership.html
Library, the Navy Department—Web Site of the Navy Department Library
  http://www.history.navy.mil/library/

LIFELines
   http://www.lifelines.navy.mil/
Lodges, Navy
   http://www.navy-lodge.com/
Low Frequency Active (LFA) Scientific Research Program
   http://www.surtass-lfa-eis.com/

M

Mailing Addresses
   http://www.chinfo.navy.mil/navpalib/ships/lists/ship-fpo.html
Maintenance, Ships
   http://www.navsea.navy.mil/innovation_template.asp?txt-
   DataID=8959
Mammal Program, Navy's Marine
   http://www.spawar.navy.mil/sandiego/technology/
   mammals/
Marine Corps—The Web Site of the U.S. Marine Corps
   http://www.usmc.mil/
Marine Corps News Service
   http://www.chinfo.navy.mil/navpalib/news/mcnews/.www/
   mcnews.html
Maritime Administration, U.S.
   http://www.marad.dot.gov/
MARS—Navy–Marine Corps MARS Telecommunications
   System National Home Page
   http://navymars.org/
Master Chief Petty Officer of the Navy
   http://www.chinfo.navy.mil/navpalib/mcpon/mcponpg.html
Master Chief Petty Officer of the Navy Leadership, Management,
   and Personal Growth Reading List (updated August 2001)
   http://www.chinfo.navy.mil/navpalib/mcpon/readgide2.
   html
Master Chief Petty Officer of the Navy, Newsletter of the—Direct Line
   http://www.persnet.navy.mil/mcpon/directline/
Master Chief Petty Officer of the Navy Required Reading Lists
   http://www.chinfo.navy.mil/navpalib/mcpon/readgide.html
MCPON Minute
   http://www.chinfo.navy.mil/navpalib/mcpon/minutes/
   minutes01.html

Medal of Honor Citations from the U.S. Army Center for Military History
http://www.army.mil/cmh-pg/moh1.htm

Medals and Awards, How to Check on
http://www.chinfo.navy.mil/navpalib/questions/awards.html

Medals and Ribbons, Navy
http://www.chinfo.navy.mil/navpalib/ribbons/
navy_ribbons.html

Medals, U.S. Navy Service and Campaign—From the Naval Historical Web Site
http://www.history.navy.mil/medals/index.html

Medicine and Surgery, Bureau of
http://navymedicine.med.navy.mil/

Medical News, Navy and Marine Corps
http://www.chinfo.navy.mil/navpalib/news/mednews/
.www/mednews.html

Memorial, U.S. Navy
http://www.lonesailor.org/

Meteorology and Oceanography Command, Naval, Newsletter—NMOC News Online
http://pao.cnmoc.navy.mil/pao/n_online/frntpage.htm

Meteorology and Oceanography Command, Naval—Weather and Ocean Information
http://pao.cnmoc.navy.mil/

MIA/POW database—From the Library of Congress Web Site
http://lcweb2.loc.gov/pow/powhome.html

Mission statement, Navy's
http://www.chinfo.navy.mil/navpalib/organization/org-top.
html

Military Terms, Dictionary of
http://www.dtic.mil/doctrine/jel/doddict/

Moving—Household Goods, etc.
http://207.132.136.34/navsuphhg/index.htm

Museum, Hampton Roads Naval
http://www.hrnm.navy.mil/hrnm1.html

Museum, National Air and Space
http://www.nasm.si.edu/

Museum of Naval Aviation, National
http://www.naval-air.org/

Museum, Navy, Washington, D.C.
http://www.history.navy.mil/branches/nhcorg8.htm

Music, Ceremonial—Marches and Selected Music Performed
by the U.S. Navy Band
http://www.bupers.navy.mil/navymusic/audio.htm
MyPay—Military Pay Site
https://mypay.dfas.mil/mypay.asp

N

Nautilus, USS—First Nuclear-Powered Submarine Museum
http://www.ussnautilus.org/
Naval Home—Web Site of the U.S. Naval Home
http://www.afrh.gov/afrh/gulfport/afrhgulfport.htm
Naval Institute Press
http://www.usni.org/webstore/shopdisplaybooks.asp?
Search=Yes
Naval Institute, U.S.
http://www.usni.org/
Naval Power 21—A Naval Vision
http://www.chinfo.navy.mil/navpalib/people/secnav/
england/navpow21.pdf
Naval Vessel Register—The Official Inventory of U.S. Naval
Ships and Service Craft
http://www.nvr.navy.mil/
Navy Electronic Commerce Online (NECO)
http://www.neco.navy.mil/
NavyOnLine—The Gateway to Navy Web Sites
http://www.ncts.navy.mil/nol/
NewsStand, Navy—Daily News from the Navy
http://www.news.navy.mil/

O

Officer Candidate School (OCS), Navy
https://www.cnet.navy.mil/nascweb/ocs/ocs.htm
Organizations with Navy Ties
http://www.chinfo.navy.mil/navpalib/people/organizations/
organizations.html

P

"Partnership . . . From the Sea," Remarks by Adm. J. M.

Boorda, 6 November 1995
   http://www.chinfo.navy.mil/navpalib/policy/fromsea/
   boor1106.txt
Pay—Defense Finance and Accounting Service (DFAS)
   http://www.dfas.mil/
Pay Charts from DFAS
   http://www.dfas.mil/money/milpay/pay/
Per Diem Rates
   http://www.dtic.mil/perdiem/pdrates.html
Personally Identifying Information from Publicly Accessible
   Web Sites, Removal of
   http://www.chinfo.navy.mil/navpalib/internet/alnav58-02.pdf
Personnel Management, Office of—Employment Opportunities with the Federal Government, Including the Department
   of the Navy
   http://jobsearch.usajobs.opm.gov/series_search.asp
Personnel Records Center, National
   http://www.archives.gov/facilities/mo/st_louis/
   military_personnel_records.html
Physical Readiness Program, Navy—Physical Fitness
   http://www.mwr.navy.mil/mwrprgms/physred.htm
Photographs/Images/Video Products, Requests for
   http://www.chinfo.navy.mil/navpalib/questions/photos.html
Policy Issues—Statements, Releases, etc.
   http://www.chinfo.navy.mil/navpalib/policy/
Personnel Development Command, Naval
   http://www.npdc.navy.mil/
Postgraduate School, Naval
   http://www.nps.navy.mil/
Posture Statement, Navy—1994 Edition
   http://www.chinfo.navy.mil/navpalib/policy/postur94/
   .www/posture.html
Posture Statement, Navy—1997: Enduring Impact . . . From
   the Sea
   http://www.chinfo.navy.mil/navpalib/policy/fromsea/
   pos97/pos-top.html
Posture Statement, Navy—1998: Forward . . . From the Sea:
   Anytime, Anywhere
   http://www.chinfo.navy.mil/navpalib/policy/fromsea/
   pos98/pos-top.html
Posture Statement, Navy—1999 Edition
   http://www.chinfo.navy.mil/navpalib/policy/fromsea/

pos99/pos-top.html

Posture Statement, Navy—2000 Edition
http://www.chinfo.navy.mil/navpalib/policy/fromsea/
pos00/pos-top.html

Posture Statement, Navy—2002 Edition: Naval Power 21: A
Naval Vision
http://www.chinfo.navy.mil/navpalib/people/secnav/
england/navpow21.pdf

POW/MIA Database—From the Library of Congress Web Site
http://lcweb2.loc.gov/pow/powhome.html

Privacy Act Online Resource Center—From the Department of
the Navy Privacy Act Office
http://privacy.navy.mil/

Program Guide to the U.S. Navy—1998 edition
http://www.chinfo.navy.mil/navpalib/policy/vision/
vis98/top-vpp.html

Program Guide to the U.S. Navy—1999 Edition
http://www.chinfo.navy.mil/navpalib/policy/vision/
vis99/top-v99.html

Program Guide to the U.S. Navy—2000 Edition
http://www.chinfo.navy.mil/navpalib/policy/vision/
vis00/top-v00.html

Program Guide to the U.S. Navy—2002 Edition
http://www.chinfo.navy.mil/navpalib/policy/vision/
vis02/top-v02.html

Programs Office, Navy International
https://www.nipo.navy.mil/

Promotions—Current Lists from Navy Personnel Command
Web Site
http://www.persnet.navy.mil/selectbd/index.html

Public Affairs Centers, Navy
http://www.chinfo.navy.mil/navpalib/chinfo/pacens.html

Public Affairs Directory
http://www.chinfo.navy.mil/navpalib/chinfo/paodir/

Q

Quality of Life Mall—LIFELines
http://www.lifelines.navy.mil/

Questions and Answers About the Navy
http://www.chinfo.navy.mil/navpalib/.www/faq.html

R

Ranks, Rates, and Ratings Insignia
   http://www.chinfo.navy.mil/navpalib/ranks/rankrate.html
Rating Insignia and Duties, Navy
   http://www.chinfo.navy.mil/navpalib/ratings/navrate.html
Recipes, Navy—Note: Feeds 100
   http://www.nll.navsup.navy.mil/recipe/display.cfm
Records, Personnel—National Personnel Records Center
   http://www.archives.gov/facilities/mo/st_louis/
   military_personnel_records.html
Recruiting Command, Navy
   http://www.navy.com/index.jsp
Reserve Recruiting Command, Naval
   http://www.navy-reserve-jobs.com/
Red Cross, American
   http://www.redcross.org/
Relief Society, Navy–Marine Corps
   http://www.nmcrs.org/
Reserve Force, Commander, Naval
   http://reserves.navy.mil
Reserve Direct Commission Officer Course
   https://www.cnet.navy.mil/nascweb/dco/dco.htm
Reserve Officers' Training Corps, Navy (NROTC)
   https://www.nrotc.navy.mil/
Reserve Recruiting Command, Naval
   http://www.navy-reserve-jobs.com/
Retired Pay Information from DFAS Web Site
   http://www.dfas.mil/money/retired/
Retirees—Shift Colors: The Newsletter for Navy
   http://www.persnet.navy.mil/periodicals/shiftcolors/

S

Safety—Naval Safety Center, Norfolk, Virginia
   http://www.safetycenter.navy.mil/
Sail200—USS *Constitution* Under Sail for the First Time in
   116 years
   http://www.chinfo.navy.mil/navpalib/ships/constitution/
   sail200b.html

Sailors, Civil War Database—From the National Park Service
http://www.itd.nps.gov/cwss/sailors_index.html

Sailor's Creed
http://www.chinfo.navy.mil/navpalib/traditions/html/
sailorscreed.html

SALTS—Web Site for the Streamlined Automated Logistics
Transmission System
http://www.salts.navy.mil/

Salvage—Recovery Operations of Aircraft, Which Have
Crashed at Sea
http://www.chinfo.navy.mil/navpalib/oceanography/
sar.html

Science and Technology Focus Site for Students and Teachers,
Office of Naval Research's
http://www.onr.navy.mil/focus/ocean/

Seabees Fact Sheet
http://www.chinfo.navy.mil/navpalib/factfile/personnel/
seabees/seabee1.html

Sea Cadets, Naval—Navy/Coast Guard Youth Training Program (Personal Note: The author is a former Sea Cadet.)
http://www.seacadets.org/

SEALs
http://www.seal.navy.mil/

SEALs Fact File Page
http://www.chinfo.navy.mil/navpalib/factfile/personnel/
seals/seals.html

Search the Navy Web Site
http://www.chinfo.navy.mil/search/

Seawolf—Releases, Remarks
http://www.chinfo.navy.mil/navpalib/ships/submarines/
seawolf/

Secretaries of the Navy, List of
http://www.chinfo.navy.mil/navpalib/people/secnav/
secnavs.html

Secretary of the Navy
http://www.chinfo.navy.mil/navpalib/people/secnav/
secnavpg.html

Secretary of the Navy—The Honorable Hansford T. Johnson, Acting Secretary of the Navy: 7 February 2003–1 October 2003
http://www.chinfo.navy.mil/navpalib/people/secnav/
johnsonht/johnson-acting.html

Secretary of the Navy—The Honorable Susan Morissey Livingston, Acting Secretary: 24 January 2003–7 February 2003
http://www.chinfo.navy.mil/navpalib/people/secnav/livingston/secnavpg-liv.html

Secretary of the Navy—The Honorable Gordon R. England, SECNAV: 24 May 2001–24 January 2003
http://www.chinfo.navy.mil/navpalib/people/secnav/england/englandpg.html

Secretary of the Navy—The Honorable Robert B. Pirie Jr., Acting Secretary: 20 January 2001–24 May 2001
http://www.chinfo.navy.mil/navpalib/people/secnav/pirie/pirie-page.html

Secretary of the Navy—The Honorable Richard Danzig, SECNAV: 16 November 1998–20 January 2001
http://www.chinfo.navy.mil/navpalib/people/secnav/danzig/

Secretary of the Navy—The Honorable John H. Dalton, SECNAV: 22 July 1993–16 November 1998
http://www.chinfo.navy.mil/navpalib/people/secnav/dalton/daltonpg.html

Selection Board information—From the BUPERS Web Site
http://www.persnet.navy.mil/selectbd/index.html

Service Craft—The Official Inventory from the Naval Vessel Register
http://www.nvr.navy.mil/nvrservicecraft/index.htm

Shift Colors—The Newsletter for Navy Retirees
http://www.persnet.navy.mil/periodicals/shiftcolors/

SHIPMAIN—NAVSEA's Ship Maintenance Process
http://www.navsea.navy.mil/innovation_template.asp?txt-DataID=8959

Ships, Alphabetical List—By Ships' Names
http://www.chinfo.navy.mil/navpalib/ships/lists/shipalfa.html

Shore Facilities, Naval
http://www.chinfo.navy.mil/navpalib/bases/navbases.html

Signal Flags
http://www.chinfo.navy.mil/navpalib/communications/flags/flags.html

Small and Disadvantaged Business Utilization—Office of the Secretary of the Navy
http://www.hq.navy.mil/sadbu/default.htm

Smallpox Immunization Program
   http://www.smallpox.army.mil/
SMART Transcripts—Sailor/Marine American Council on Education Registry Transcript (SMART)
   https://smart.cnet.navy.mil/
Soldiers' and Sailors' Relief Act
   http://www.chinfo.navy.mil/navpalib/questions/ssrelief/usc50top.html
Space Available Travel Information—From the Air Mobility Command, USAF
   http://public.amc.af.mil/SPACEA/spacea.htm
Speaker's Bureau, Navy—How to Obtain a Navy Speaker for Your Event
   http://www.chinfo.navy.mil/navpalib/chinfo/speakers.html
Speeches—Chief of Naval Operations
   http://www.chinfo.navy.mil/navpalib/cno/clark-speeches.html
Speeches—Secretary of the Navy
   http://www.chinfo.navy.mil/navpalib/people/secnav/secnavpg.html#speeches
Speeches—Under Secretary of the Navy
   http://www.chinfo.navy.mil/navpalib/people/undersec/undersec.html
Specifications and Standards—The DoD Index of Specifications and Standards. A searchable list of unclassified Federal and Military specifications, standards, and related standardization documents
   http://stinet.dtic.mil/str/dodiss4_fields.html
Staff Corps Officers' Specialty Insignia
   http://www.chinfo.navy.mil/navpalib/ranks/officers/specialty-staff/spclstaff.html
Standard Navy Distribution List, What Is the
   http://www.chinfo.navy.mil/navpalib/questions/sndl-web.html
Standard Navy Distribution List, OPNAV Notice 5400—Latest Version
   http://neds.nebt.daps.mil/sndl.htm
Submarines
   http://www.chinfo.navy.mil/navpalib/ships/submarines/
Submarine Warfare Division—N77
   http://www.chinfo.navy.mil/navpalib/cno/n87/n77.html

Suggestions, Beneficial (BeneSugs), The Instruction Concerning
http://neds.nebt.daps.mil/Directives/1650c8.pdf
Surface Warfare Directorate—N76
http://www.chinfo.navy.mil/navpalib/cno/n76/
Surface Warfare Magazine—The Official Magazine of the U.S.
Surface Fleet
http://www.navsea.navy.mil/swmagazine/
Surplus Equipment—How to Buy Information from the Defense Reutilization and Marketing Service
http://www.drms.dla.mil/

T

Task Force EXCEL—CNO's Initiative to Revolutionize Navy
Training
http://www.excel.navy.mil/
Television Show, Navy–Marine Corps News—Current Edition
http://www.news.navy.mil/search/nmcnlist.asp
Terminology, Origins of Navy
http://www.chinfo.navy.mil/navpalib/traditions/html/
navyterm.html
Terms, Dictionary of Military
http://www.dtic.mil/doctrine/jel/doddict/
Testimony
http://www.chinfo.navy.mil/navpalib/testimony/
testimon.html
Time—USNO Master Clock Time
http://tycho.usno.navy.mil/what.html
Transcripts—Sailor/Marine American Council on Education
Registry Transcript (SMART)
https://smart.cnet.navy.mil/
Transportal, Department of Defense
http://www.dodtransportal.org/dodtransportal/
Transportation Incentive Program
http://www.chinfo.navy.mil/navpalib/transportation/
alnav038-01.txt
TriCare
http://www.tricare.osd.mil/
TWA Flight 800 Recovery Efforts
http://www.chinfo.navy.mil/navpalib/oceanography/
twacrash.html

U

Undersecretary of the Navy
   http://www.chinfo.navy.mil/navpalib/people/undersec/
   undersec.html
Undersecretaries of the Navy, Past
   http://www.chinfo.navy.mil/navpalib/people/undersec/
   undersecnavs.html
Undersea Warfare Magazine—The Official Magazine of the
   U.S. Navy Submarine Force
   http://www.chinfo.navy.mil/navpalib/cno/n87/mag.html
Uniform Regulations, U.S. Navy—From NAVPERS Web Site
   [PDF file]
   https://buperscd.technology.navy.mil/bup_updt/508/unireg/
   uregMenu.html
USO
   http://www.uso.org/pubs/8_13_18.cfm?CFID=2005587&
   CFTOKEN=66450912

V

Vaccinations for the Military
   http://www.vaccines.army.mil/default.asp
Vessel Register Battleship List, Naval
   http://www.nvr.navy.mil/nvrships/s_BB.htm
Veterans Affairs, Department of
   http://www.va.gov/
Vessel Register, Naval—The Official Inventory of U.S. Naval
   Ships
   http://www.nvr.navy.mil/nvrships/index.htm
Veterans' Benefits
   http://www.chinfo.navy.mil/navpalib/people/faq/.www/
   veterans.html
Video of the Navy, Digital
   http://www.chinfo.navy.mil/navpalib/videos/videos.html
Video Products, Requests for
   http://www.chinfo.navy.mil/navpalib/questions/photos.html
Vieques Island—The Honorable Robert B. Pirie, Jr., Undersecretary of the Navy, provides the facts concerning Vieques at
   the National Image Salute to Hispanic-Americans in the Military Banquet in Atlantic City, New Jersey, 24 May 2001

http://www.chinfo.navy.mil/navpalib/people/secnav/pirie/
speeches/pirie010524.txt

Vieques news release—18 October 1999
http://www.chinfo.navy.mil/navpalib/news/news_stories/
vieques1018.html

Voting—Navy Voting Assistance Program
http://www.persnet.navy.mil/nvap/

W

War College, Naval, Newport, Rhode Island
http://www.nwc.navy.mil/

Wardrobe, Rainbow—The Colors Worn by Flight Deck Personnel
http://www.chinfo.navy.mil/navpalib/ships/carriers/
rainbow.html

Warrant Officers' Specialty Insignia
http://www.chinfo.navy.mil/navpalib/ranks/officers/ldo-warrant/ldo-war.html

Waste, Fraud and Abuse Hotline, DoD
http://dodig.osd.mil/hotline/

Web Site Accessibility [Section 508], Navy
http://www.chinfo.navy.mil/navpalib/accessibility/

Web Site Administration, Policies and Procedures, Department
of Defense
http://www.defenselink.mil/webmasters/policy/
dod_web_policy_12071998_with_amendments_and_
corrections.html

Whales, 14 June 2000, Navy Assisting in Determining Stranding of
http://www.chinfo.navy.mil/navpalib/news/news_stories/
whales.html

What's New—In This Web Site over the Past Month
http://www.chinfo.navy.mil/navpalib/.www/whatsnew.html

Why the Aircraft Carrier
http://www.chinfo.navy.mil/navpalib/ships/carriers/cv-why.html

Wire Service, Navy
http://www.chinfo.navy.mil/navpalib/news/navywire/
.www/navywire.html

Women in the Navy—Numbers, Firsts, Statements, etc.

http://www.chinfo.navy.mil/navpalib/people/women/
wintop.html
World War II—D-Day speeches, etc.
http://www.chinfo.navy.mil/navpalib/wwii/events/dday/
World War II—Events of Remembrance—Remarks, etc.
http://www.chinfo.navy.mil/navpalib/wwii/events/
World War II—Facts on Various Aspects of WWII
http://www.chinfo.navy.mil/navpalib/wwii/facts/
World War II—News Releases
http://www.chinfo.navy.mil/navpalib/wwii/news/

Y

Year of the Ocean, International
http://www.chinfo.navy.mil/navpalib/oceanography/
yoto1998.html

Part Three

Touchstones

Birth of Tradition 20

From *Almanac of Naval Facts, United States Naval Institute, 1964*

Today the United States possesses the largest and most capable Navy in the world, and has since the end of World War II. Some two hundred years ago, however, when the nation was young, that wasn't so—and the world's newest and smallest Navy fought superpowers and pirates in the name of freedom. The Navy fought for the nation's right to exist and for freedom of the seas. It was in that time that the traditions and the proud heritage of the U.S. Navy were forged. Following are brief accounts of the U.S. naval engagements from the Revolutionary War through the end of the War of 1812.

First Sea Battle of the American Revolution (12 June 1775)

Though there was no American Navy at the time, this was the first clash occurring on the water. The British cutter *Margaretta,* entering the harbor of Machias, Maine, with two sloops to commandeer a load of lumber for Gen. Thomas Gage's army at Boston, was challenged by Jeremiah O'Brien, leading a group of lumberjacks and fellow townsmen brandishing pitchforks. *Margaretta* stood out into the stream, whereupon O'Brien seized *Unity,* one of the sloops, and went after her. The Maine men pitted rifles against cannon, used stacks of lumber as bulwarks, and picked off British gunners through *Margaretta*'s ports. In thirty minutes O'Brien's men killed the midshipman skipper of the enemy ship, boarded her, and ran up a homemade white flag bearing a green pine tree and the legend "An Appeal to Heaven." (Note: One of the few remaining Liberty Ships from World War II is named after Jeremiah

O'Brien and is the focal point of the National Liberty Ship Memorial in San Francisco, California. More information can be found at http://www.ssjeremiahobrien.org/)

Lee versus *Nancy* (29 November 1775)

Capt. John Manly, Marblehead fisherman and former boatswain's mate in the Royal Navy, was sailing in *Lee,* a four-gun schooner, under orders from Gen. George Washington. While cruising off Massachusetts for the purpose of intercepting supplies destined for the British army, he took the British *Nancy.* Her cargo included 2,000 muskets with bayonets, 8,000 fuzes, 31 tons of musket shot, 3,000 24-pound round shot, several barrels of powder, 2 cannon, and a 13-inch mortar described as "the noblest piece of ordnance ever landed in America." These supplies proved most valuable to the Continental Army. General Washington used the cannon when forcing the British to evacuate Boston four months later.

Attack on New Providence, Bahamas (3–4 March 1776)

First amphibious assault launched by the U.S. Navy. Almost every ship the Navy had was involved. U.S. Marines first saw combat under the leadership of Comdr. Esek Hopkins. Capt. Samuel Nicholas led 250 Marines ashore from the fleet, combined them with 50 Sailors under *Cabot*'s Lieutenant Weaver, and captured Nassau, New Providence, Bahamas, with only slight resistance and no bloodshed. Though Marines and Sailors captured eighty-eight cannon, fifteen mortars, and twenty-four casks of gunpowder, the island's British governor was able to spirit away most of his munitions on the night of 3 March in a merchant schooner. After holding the island for two weeks, the fleet sailed for Rhode Island, taking the governor and other officials with them as hostages.

American Turtle versus *Eagle* (7 September 1776)

Sgt. Esra Lee of the Continental Army, piloting a one-man submarine devised by David Bushnell, approached the enemy warship in New York Harbor with the intention of fastening a "time bomb," or mine, to her hull. Due to *Eagle*'s bottom being copper-plated, however, Lee's attempt was unsuccessful. The mine was set adrift and exploded without damage. This was the first American submarine attack on an enemy warship. (Note: The Connecticut River Museum in Essex, Connecticut, has a working model of the submarine *Turtle*. More information can be found at http://www.ctrivermuseum.org/turtle.htm)

First Battle of Lake Champlain (11–13 October 1776)

Brig. Gen. Benedict Arnold led a force of one sloop, three schooners, eight gondolas, and four galleys, mounting ninety-four cannon and manned by about 700 men, against a British force of twenty-nine vessels. Arnold's "navy" was defeated, but the time they had caused the British army to consume in building a fleet to win control of the lake proved valuable. British forces shortly thereafter became so scattered in various campaigns that they could not combine to cut off New England from the rest of the colonies, as they had hoped to do earlier by taking Lake Champlain and controlling the Hudson River.

Alfred versus *Mellish* (12 November 1776)

While cruising in company with *Providence* (Capt. Hoysted Hacker), the twenty-four-gun ship *Alfred,* under Capt. John Paul Jones, captured the British transport *Mellish* and 150 prisoners. The British cargo included 10,000 suits of winter uniform, destined for Gen. John Burgoyne's army at Montreal, Canada. While convoying *Mellish* and seven other prizes into port, *Alfred,* having parted company with *Providence,* encountered the British frigate *Milford.* Jones drew the enemy warship off while his prizes ran for shore, then, having made sure the Englishman was too far away to chase them, loosed all sail and slipped away. He joined his prizes later off Nantasket, Massachusetts, and brought them safe into port, where the uniforms were transferred to the Continental Army.

Ranger versus *Drake* (24 April 1778)

After having raided Whitehaven, England, in the *Ranger,* John Paul Jones put into the harbor of Carrickfergus, where the British warship *Drake* lay moored, taking on supplies. After waiting for the enemy to come to quarters, Jones opened fire. Within thirty minutes *Drake*'s captain lay dying, and forty of her crew were dead. *Ranger* lost six men in the battle, during which Jones fought the enemy while putting down a mutiny on his own ship. This was the first defeat of a British warship by an American naval vessel.

Bonhomme Richard versus *Serapis* (23 September 1779)

The *Bonhomme Richard,* forty-two guns, under John Paul Jones, acting with three ships under French captains, sighted the British ships *Serapis* and *Countess of Scarborough* escorting a merchant convoy off Flamborough Head, England. Jones engaged the *Serapis,* a frigate of fifty guns, and the French *Pallas* captured the *Countess of Scarborough* after a two-hour battle. The two remaining French ships gave no assistance, and the convoy fled. When *Bonhomme Richard* fired her first broadside, two of her lower deck cannons exploded, killing the gun crews. The men refused to fire any more of these guns, and Jones was left with only small cannon on the upper deck. When *Bonhomme Richard* was being rapidly destroyed, Jones lashed her alongside the *Serapis* and sent men into the rigging to fire on the enemy. *Bonhomme Richard* was on fire and leaking badly, when one of the gunners cried for quarter and attempted to haul down the colors. Jones killed him by throwing a pistol at his head. Captain Pearson of the *Serapis* asked Jones if he had surrendered. Jones replied, "Surrender? I have not yet begun to fight!" Jones's master-at-arms, seeing the fires and the leaks, thought his ship was sinking and so released all prisoners. The English would have turned on the U.S. crew but were told both ships were sinking and that they must man *Bonhomme Richard*'s pumps to save their own lives.

Meanwhile, Jones's men in the rigging had climbed over into the masts of *Serapis.* One of them dropped a grenade, which fell down an open hatch of *Serapis* and started a powder fire. At this point *Alliance,* under the French captain Landais, entered the engagement by firing broadsides into both *Bonhomme Richard* and *Serapis.* As Pearson could not see that *Alliance* was damaging *Bonhomme Richard* as much as *Serapis,* he thought that further fighting was useless and surrendered. The battle lasted three and one-half hours. As *Bonhomme Richard* was sinking, Jones transferred his prisoners and crew to *Serapis.* This is the only instance in which the victor lost his own ship and returned to port in the ship he captured.

Alliance versus *Atalanta* and *Trepassy* (29 May 1781)

While en route home after landing *Lafayette* in France, Capt. John Barry's thirty-two-gun ship *Alliance* met *Atalanta* and *Trepassy* on a calm day with little wind. *Atalanta* had twenty guns and 130 men, while her consort mounted fourteen guns and had an eighty-man crew. Though wounded early in the battle, Barry rallied his men and, taking advantage of a slight wind, ran between the enemy ships and gave each a broadside. This lessened his enemies' zeal considerably, for they surrendered shortly afterward.

Hyder Ally versus *General Monk* (8 April 1782)

General Monk had formerly been the Continental ship *George Washington,* captured by the British in the occupation of Philadelphia, and had more than sixty captures of American ships to her credit. With four other British ships, she sighted the Pennsylvania-owned *Hyder Ally,* sixteen guns, under Joshua Barney, escorting a fleet of merchantmen through the mouth of the Delaware River. *General Monk* stood in alone to take what looked like an easy prey, but Barney (by having his helmsman follow the "rule of contrary") lured the Englishman alongside. Barney ordered his steersman to turn left, whereupon the British ship followed suit in order to stay parallel for a broadside. *Hyder Ally* turned right, instead, and fouled her jib in *General Monk*'s rigging. The enemy's guns were pointed into empty space, while *Hyder Ally*'s could rake her opponent's decks. *General Monk* surrendered in thirty minutes, and Barney dashed upstream with his prize before other British ships realized what had happened.

Delaware versus *Croyable* (9 July 1798)

While cruising along the Atlantic coast in USS *Delaware,* twenty guns, Capt. Stephen Decatur Sr. sighted four schooners. Decatur stood off, pretending he was a merchantman anxious to avoid them, and one schooner gave chase. Decatur let the Frenchman approach, then suddenly turned to give battle. The Frenchman, discovering he was facing a warship, attempted to escape, but a few rounds from *Delaware*'s guns forced his surrender. The French ship was the *Croyable,* fourteen guns. Taken into Philadelphia, she was renamed USS *Retaliation.* For this capture Decatur and his men received the first prize money awarded men of the "new" Navy.

Constellation versus *Insurgente* (9 February 1799)

Constellation was launched on 7 September 1797, just prior to the entry of the United States into its first naval war. The "Quasi War" (1798–1801) with France was largely *Constellation*'s war. On 9 February 1799 *Constellation* fought and captured the thirty-six-gun frigate *L'Insurgente,* the fastest ship in the French navy. Under the command of the Capt. Thomas Truxtun, it was the first battle by one of the original six frigates. This was the first major victory by an American-designed and American-built warship.

Constellation versus *Vengeance* (1–2 February 1800)

Captain Truxton won another victory in a running battle, almost yardarm to yardarm on parallel courses, during which *Vengeance* struck her colors, then escaped in the darkness because the Americans could not see that she had surrendered. *Vengeance* received 160 battle casualties, *Constellation* thirty-nine.

Destruction of *Philadelphia* (16 February 1804)

While pursuing a pirate vessel into the harbor of Tripoli on 31 October 1803, Capt. William Bainbridge's thirty-six-gun frigate went aground and all hands were captured by the pirates. Because *Philadelphia* posed a threat to the blockading American squadron by augmenting pirate shore batteries, Captain Bainbridge managed to smuggle out a letter written in lemon juice to Capt. Edward Preble, suggesting that a small ship slip in at night, board the frigate, and burn her. Lt. Stephen Decatur, who had just captured the Tripolitan ketch *Mastico* and renamed her USS *Intrepid,* volunteered for the venture. With seventy-four officers and men from USS *Enterprise* and *Constitution,* Decatur ran alongside *Philadel-*

phia in the darkness, boarded and set her afire, then withdrew under fire from shore batteries with only one man wounded. *Philadelphia* burned, exploded, and sank. Horatio, Lord Nelson, called Decatur's exploit "the most bold and daring act of the age."

Bombardment of Tripoli Harbor (3 August–3 September 1804)

During this period, a U.S. squadron under Comdr. Edward Preble made five attacks on the pirate stronghold. Ships involved at first were *Constitution,* flagship; three sixteen-gun brigs, *Argus, Scourge,* and *Siren;* three twelve-gun schooners, *Vixen, Nautilus,* and *Enterprise;* two mortar-carrying bomb vessels; and six gunboats. These mounted 156 guns and were manned by 1,060 men. Opposing them were 115 shore guns, plus one brig, two schooners, two galleys, and nineteen gunboats. Total enemy guns were 227, and Tripolitan forces numbered 25,000 men. On 7 August USS *John Adams* joined the U.S. squadron. While maneuvering carefully to avoid boarding, American ships sank three enemy gunboats and captured four, while suffering only fifty-four casualties. This was the first effective action taken against the Tripolitan pirates and had a great effect on the execution of a treaty some months later.

Chesapeake versus *Leopard* (22 June 1807)

Having been ordered to duty in the Mediterranean, Capt. James Barron put to sea on 21 June, planning to train his hurriedly gathered crew and mount his guns while crossing the Atlantic. The next day, just outside U.S. waters, he was hailed by the fifty-gun British frigate *Leopard.* Though not prepared for battle, Barron refused to let the British search his ship for English-born seamen, whereupon *Leopard* fired a broadside that killed three U.S. Sailors and wounded eighteen others, including Captain Barron. During the next fifteen minutes, Barron was able to fire only one token shot before hauling down the American colors. A boarding party from *Leopard* boarded *Chesapeake* and seized four men who claimed to be British deserters. The aftermath of this incident was the court-martial and five-year suspension of Captain Barron for not having his ship battle-ready and an embargo against Great Britain.

President versus *Little Belt* (16 May 1811)

While cruising from Annapolis to New York, Capt. John Rodgers received word from a coasting vessel that an American seaman had been impressed into a British warship near Sandy Hook. Next day he sighted a sail and closed in to hail the ship, which he recognized as British, but whose strength he could not measure in the poor weather. At his second hail, the British opened fire. Broadsides were exchanged, but when Rodgers saw that the enemy ship was smaller than his, he stood off to await her next move. Two thirty-two-pound shot then crashed into his mainmast, and *President* returned to action and silenced the English guns.

After lying alongside all night, Rodgers sent a boat to the other ship in the morning and learned she was the eighteen-gun sloop-of-war *Little Belt,* with nine British crewmen dead, twenty-two wounded. *Little Belt* limped into Halifax, and *President* continued cruising. This is the American version of the incident. The British version differed completely, and resentment on both sides of the Atlantic was so great that many U.S. cities began making preparations for war. When President Madison stated that U.S. warships had the right to challenge foreign vessels near her shores, and simultaneously presented proof the British were operating an espionage ring in this country, the matter was closed.

President versus *Belvedere* (23 June 1812)

While cruising off the Atlantic coast as flagship of a squadron that included *United States, Congress,* and *Argus,* Captain Rodgers's frigate sighted an English warship. The entire squadron gave chase, but only *President,* being fastest, caught up. Her first three shots smashed in *Belvedere*'s stern, and as the American gunners prepared to fire a few more shots from their long guns, they were confident that the battle would be a short and victorious one. On the fourth shot, a bow chaser exploded, killing or wounding eighteen men and breaking Captain Rodgers's leg. Rodgers hoped to disable the English ship before she could damage his ship extensively, but the enemy kept cutting away rigging, jettisoning material, and repairing damage at a great rate. By nightfall Captain Byron of *Belvedere* had thrown over his spare anchor, barge, yawl, and jolly boat, while pumping fourteen tons of water from *Belvedere*'s hold. This had the desired effect, and she gained way on *President*. By 2350, seeing further pursuit was useless, Rodgers broke off the chase. *Belvedere* escaped into Halifax.

Essex versus *Alert* (13 August 1812)

While cruising in USS *Essex,* thirty-two guns, Capt. David Porter sighted a British warship and used the popular device of pretending to be a merchant ship to draw the enemy within range. The eighteen-gun ship *Alert,* under Capt. Thomas Laugharne, sped in on *Essex*'s quarter and opened fire as her crew gave three cheers. Then the gun ports on *Essex* flew open, and a broadside slammed into *Alert*. This was followed in rapid succession by further attacks, and in eight minutes *Alert* surrendered, ending the first conclusive naval action of the War of 1812.

Constitution versus *Guerrière* (19 August 1812)

Because enemy shot caromed off her thick bulkheads, *Constitution,* under Captain Isaac Hull, won her nickname "Old Ironsides" in this battle. She met the British warship, *Guerrière,* about 700 miles off Boston, and in thirty minutes reduced her to a helpless wreck. Capt. James R. Dacres, of *Guerrière,* had previously been an arrogant man and had offered to bet a new hat that he could defeat within fifteen minutes any ship the Americans could produce. Upon surrendering, he offered his sword to the victor. Hull declined it, adding, "But if you don't mind, Captain, I'll trouble you for your hat."

Wasp versus *Frolic* (18 October 1812)

Two days out of port Capt. Jacob Jones, in USS *Wasp,* sighted and chased a sloop-of-war guarding a convoy. As the vessel came about to challenge, Jones saw her break a Spanish flag, but believed her to be running under false colors, a common practice in those days. As he closed to about sixty yards range, the sloop-of-war hauled down the Spanish flag, ran up a British flag, and fired a broadside. She had fired on an up roll, however, and her fire tore into *Wasp*'s rigging. Jones's gunners were ready, and their broadside did tremendous damage. *Wasp* hauled off and raked her enemy effectively, then stood by to observe damage because the heavy seas made any attempt at boarding dangerous to both ship and crew. Then the ships collided and Seaman Jack Lange, an American who had once been impressed by the British, leaped on board the other ship, cutlass in hand, followed by a few of his shipmates. All that confronted them was one wounded steersman and three British officers. *Wasp*'s fire had killed or wounded more than 90 of her enemy's 110-man crew, while she had only 10 casualties herself.

United States versus *Macedonian* (25 October 1812)

Off the Canary Islands, *United States,* under Capt. Stephen Decatur, encountered *Macedonian,* under Capt. John S. Carden, whose crew included seven impressed American seamen. *Macedonian* opened fire first, scoring hits on the American sails, but *United States*'s return volley showed her guns had a longer range. *Macedonian* then tried to use her superior speed to close, but American gunners smashed her rigging and swept her decks before she could do any damage. Thirty minutes of fighting saw the battle ended. *Macedonian* had 105 casualties, while only 7 of Decatur's men were killed or wounded.

Constitution versus *Java* (29 December 1812)

Some thirty miles off Salvador, Brazil, the speedier *Java* was able to rake *Constitution* several times as the American ship bore down to close with the enemy. Though twice wounded, Capt. William Bainbridge directed his fire until the British ship was helpless. *Constitution* stood off to repair her battered sails, then closed again, and had maneuvered into position for raking *Java* when the British ship surrendered. *Java* had 60 killed and 170 wounded; *Constitution* had merely 34 casualties.

Hornet versus *Peacock* (24 February 1813)

Off the coast of South America, Capt. Stephen Lawrence's eighteen-gun ship encountered the twenty-two-gun British brig, and, after maneuvering for position for more than an hour, they exchanged broadsides. *Peacock*'s shots were high, while *Hornet*'s caught her enemy in the lower rigging. Lawrence then took advantage of his own better conditions and moved to the enemy's starboard quarter. In fifteen minutes *Peacock,* sinking, surrendered.

The British vessel had thirty-eight killed and wounded, including her captain, William Peake. *Hornet* lost four men, three of whom were drowned along with nine *Peacock* men when the enemy ship suddenly sank during rescue operations. Three other Americans were wounded.

Chesapeake versus *Shannon* (1 June 1813)

Despite the story that the American ship sailed out of Boston to answer a British challenge, Capt. Stephen Lawrence left port without ever having received the letter sent him by British captain Philip Broke. He did, however, sail with the knowledge he would likely have to go into battle with inexperienced officers and men. The thirty-five-gun British frigate was far more prepared for battle. Broke had commanded *Shannon* for six years, and his crew had been with him for five. Unlike most naval officers of his day, he held daily gunnery practice and gave a prize of tobacco to the best musket marksman.

Against such well-trained men, *Chesapeake* never had a chance.

Battle commenced about 1800, and the double-shotted guns of the British did terrible damage. Marksmen in her tops shot down three *Chesapeake* helmsmen, one after another. In fifteen minutes the battle was over, with Captain Lawrence fatally wounded and the British boarding party in control. As he was being carried below, Lawrence called out, "Don't give up the ship!" Casualties in *Chesapeake* were twenty-four killed and fifty wounded. *Shannon* lost forty-seven killed and ninety-nine wounded.

Argus versus *Pelican* (14 August 1813)

In less than ten months the sixteen-gun American brig *Argus* captured or destroyed twenty-two British ships. Under Master Commandant Arthur Sinclair, she took five. The other seventeen were taken by *Argus* under Master Commandant William Henry Allen.

Argus sighted *Pelican* early in the morning. The battle began at 0600; Sinclair and his first lieutenant were wounded soon thereafter, and Lt. William Howard Allen took command. English shot quickly wrecked *Argus*'s rigging and her wheel ropes; then they stood off and poured broadside after broadside into the motionless ship. Lieutenant Allen led one last attempt to board the enemy ship, but it was easily driven back and *Argus* had to surrender. *Argus* casualties totaled a fifth of her crew, while *Pelican* lost two killed and five wounded.

Enterprise versus *Boxer* (5 September 1813)

Enterprise, fourteen guns, engaged the fourteen-gun British brig off Portland, Maine. In a twenty-minute action, the American ship received one hit to the enemy's eighteen. *Boxer* counted forty-two casualties to fourteen in *Enterprise.* The engagement was won in the first eight minutes, though the American ship did not know it. All her crew saw was that the British ship still had colors flying. After pouring shot into *Boxer* for another twelve minutes, *Enterprise* closed to hail, then found the colors were nailed in place. Both commanding officers were killed in the battle; thus, Lt. E. R. McCall, her second in command, took *Boxer* to Portland, Maine.

Battle of Lake Erie (10 September 1813)

In order to stop the British military operations in the upper Mississippi Valley, it was planned to cut off their communications with eastern Canada by obtaining control of the Great Lakes. Master Commandant Oliver H. Perry hurriedly built nine ships on Lake Erie—five of green timber. His opponent, Capt. Robert H. Barclay, built a similar fleet of six ships. On 10 September 1813, the two homemade flotillas met at the western end of the lake. On his flagship, *Lawrence,* Perry hoisted a blue flag bearing the dying words of Capt. James Lawrence, "Don't give up the ship." *Lawrence* was soon wrecked and Perry rowed in an open boat to the *Niagara* with a few survivors. He brought the rest of his ships into action then and soon won the engagement. Perry reported the victory on the back of an old letter, saying, "We have met the enemy and they are ours—two ships, two brigs, one schooner, and one sloop." This victory regained the Michigan-Detroit territory for the United States and had a marked effect on peace negotiations.

Essex versus *Phoebe* and *Cherub* (28 March 1814)

Essex, under Capt. David Porter, captured a mail packet, two schooners, and thirteen whalers on a cruise that brought her into the Pacific Ocean, the first U.S. warship to enter those waters. The havoc she wreaked on the British whaling industry soon brought retaliation, and the thirty-six-gun frigate *Phoebe,* accompanied by eighteen-gun sloop *Cherub,* trapped *Essex* in the harbor of Valparaíso, Chile.

When the British ships blockaded him, Porter led a surprise night boat attack on *Phoebe,* but called off the venture when he discovered that all the British seamen were waiting at their guns. After six weeks of being bottled up, Porter tried to make a dash out of the harbor but a sudden squall carried his topmast away. Porter ran for shore and anchored, whereupon the two enemy ships took up raking positions and opened fire. After two hours and twenty minutes Captain Porter surrendered. Of 225 *Essex* men, 58 had been killed, 66 wounded, and 31 lost by drowning. *Phoebe* had 4 killed and 7 wounded out of 300 men, while *Cherub* lost 1 man killed and 3 wounded of a 121-man crew.

Peacock versus *Epervier* (29 April 1814)

Capt. Lewis Warrington slipped his eighteen-gun sloop through the British blockade off New York and cruised down the East Coast before sighting an enemy sail off Florida. Both ships were prepared to fight and sailed straight for each other without the usual formality of a preliminary hail. *Peacock* took two thirty-two-pound shots in her fore yard with the first exchange, but her return broadside smashed most of *Epervier*'s rigging and guns. *Epervier* closed for an attempt at boarding, but another broadside, plus several volleys from U.S. Marines in *Peacock,* turned her back. American casualties were two killed and two wounded; British fifteen killed and twenty-three wounded.

This battle was hailed as a tribute to American gunnery. *Epervier* had forty-five shot holes in her port side and five feet of water in her hold when the forty-five-minute battle ended. *Peacock* received not one hit in her hull, and less than an hour after the engagement ended had repaired her rigging and was ready in all aspects to fight again.

Cruise of *Peacock* (June 1814 to June 1815)

After capturing *Epervier,* Capt. Lewis Warrington took his ship into Savannah, Georgia. Congress awarded him a gold medal, each of his officers a silver medal, and each sailing master and midshipman a sword for the capture of *Epervier* and the $125,000 in gold she had been carrying. A month later, Warrington sailed on a cruise lasting 147 days, during which *Peacock* captured or destroyed fourteen British ships, valued at $493,000, and took 150 prisoners. These actions occurred in areas as far apart as Newfoundland, Portugal, North Ireland, and the West Indies.

Last Cruise and Disappearance of *Wasp* (May–October 1814)

This sloop, named for the ship that had captured the British *Frolic* only to be taken with her prize that same evening by *Poictiers,* sailed from Portsmouth, New Hampshire, on 1 May and ranged the ocean for six months against the enemy before her mysterious disappearance. During this time she captured or sank fifteen enemy ships, two of them warships, all in English waters. Eleven of her actions, in fact, were fought in the English Channel itself.

Her most notable captures were *Reindeer* (June 28) and *Avon* (1 September). *Reindeer,* twenty-one-gun sloop, was taken nineteen minutes after *Wasp* opened fire. When the British captain, R. Williams Manner, was killed leading an attempt to board *Wasp,* his men surrendered.

Master Commandant Blakeley's crew then took a prize, *Mary,* right under the nose of the British ship of the line *Armada,* burned it, and was driven off in attempting to seize another ship *Armada* was convoying. That night *Wasp* ran down on *Avon,* a sloop of *Wasp*'s size, and after exchanging broadsides with her was about to board the enemy by boat when she sighted another enemy ship closing. *Wasp* drew away, leaving *Avon* on fire and sinking.

On 9 October, the Spanish brig *Adonis* was hailed and boarded by men who said they were from *Wasp.* After obtaining information as to the whereabouts of a British convoy, they returned to their ship. She set sail in the direction of the convoy and was never seen again.

Battle of Bladensburg (near Washington, D.C., 24 August 1814)

During the War of 1812, the British sent a strong expeditionary force into Chesapeake Bay, under Maj. Gen. Robert Rose, to operate with a British squadron under Vice Adm. Sir Alexander

Cochrane. The only American force in the bay was Capt. Joshua Barney's flotilla of twenty-six small craft manned by some 900 Sailors and Marines. Barney was soon trapped in the Patuxent River, and although he once repulsed the British, he destroyed his boats to prevent their capture. On 23 August the British began to march toward Washington. A force of about 7,000 troops under Brigadier General Winder made a small show of resistance against this force at Bladensburg, then retreated in panic. Barney, with a couple of hundred Sailors, had been joined by Capt. Samuel Miller from the Marine Barracks in Washington with a hundred Marines; this small force reached the battlefields at Bladensburg just as Winder's army began to withdraw. Three times they repulsed the superior British forces before they were flanked on both sides. Both Barney and Miller were wounded; they ordered their men to withdraw and remained behind, where they were captured by the British. With no one to stop their movements, the British marched on into Washington and set fire to several buildings before they returned to their ships.

Attack on Barataria, Gulf of Mexico
(11 September–October 1814)

With the U.S. Navy arrayed against the British fleet during the War of 1812, pirates in the Gulf of Mexico had grown increasingly bolder. Finally, a squadron of two schooners (USS *Carolina* and *Seahorse*), six gunboats, and one launch moved out from New Orleans to attack the island of Barataria, where the pirates maintained headquarters. Though the pirate force numbered about a thousand men of assorted nationalities, they burned several of their armed ships and fled as soon as the naval squadron appeared. Commander Patterson bombarded the pirate ships, captured eleven of them, and landed a force of soldiers and Marines to destroy the fort and village. The captured craft were taken back to New Orleans.

Second Battle of Lake Champlain
(11 September 1814)

In the latter part of the War of 1812, a British army of 11,000 men advanced into northern New York from Canada, relying on supplies transported from Canada by water over Lake Champlain.

The British attempted a combined land-sea attack on Plattsburg, and Master Commandant Thomas MacDonough defended the town from waterborne attack with four sailing ships and ten galleys, having a total of eighty-six guns. Opposing him, Commander Downie had four ships and twelve galleys, with a total of ninety-two guns. MacDonough's force was inferior, so he anchored his ships in such a position that the ends of his battle line were protected by harbor headlands, forcing British ships to attack head on, thus being able to use only a few guns at a time. The British ships suffered heavily in approaching and finally anchored about 500 yards from the U.S. fleet. The battle was fought at this range in smooth water.

The battle lasted two and one-half hours and ended in the capture of the entire British squadron. The loss of Lake Champlain deprived the British army of means for obtaining supplies from Canada, and it was forced to make a hasty retreat. (This is one of the few instances in history where ships at anchor won a battle.) MacDonough's report after the action read, in part, "The Lord has seen fit to grant us a signal victory."

Capture of *President* (15 January 1815)

Hoping to escape southward through the British blockade and raid enemy shipping in the East Indies, Capt. Stephen Decatur headed his forty-four-gun frigate *President* out of New York. The pilot, lacking beacon lights, ran her aground and Decatur wanted to return to harbor, but adverse wind conditions prevented this. He forced her over a sandbar and put to sea, meeting up the next day with the three-ship blockading squadron.

His damaged ship had no hope of escaping, so Decatur pointed a cannon into *President*'s hold, set a watch on it, then swiftly turned, planning to capture the leading British ship by boarding, scuttle *President,* and run for New York harbor. As he came around, however, *Endymion,* forty guns, retreated. *President* finally ran down on her at dusk and fired four broadsides that crippled the English ship.

Decatur then decided to run for New York harbor, but British reinforcements arrived. *Majestic, Pomone,* and *Tenedos* outran *President* and positioned themselves so as to keep her continually under fire. After twenty-four of his men had been killed and fifty-six wounded, Captain Decatur surrendered. Upon surrendering his sword to Capt. John Hayes, senior British officer present, it was returned to him with an expression of praise for "an officer who defended his ship so proudly."

Hornet versus *Penguin* (23 March 1815)

Master Commandant James Biddle sailed his twenty-gun sloop *Hornet* from New York on 23 January 1815, not knowing that American emissaries had attained peace earlier in London. The British nineteen-gun brig *Penguin* knew nothing of this either. Upon sighting the British ship, Biddle slowed down, waiting for her to come up, while *Penguin,* afraid her adversary would recognize her as a warship and run away, kept to a bow-on approach. At about 1340 *Penguin* was near enough to join battle. She hauled up her colors and fired a broadside, which *Hornet* answered immediately. In the ensuing action *Hornet* shot up *Penguin*'s rigging badly; *Penguin* closed and fouled her bowsprit in *Hornet*'s rigging, but for some reason made no attempt to board. Biddle, realizing he had the sailing advantage, refused to let his men leap to the enemy ship. A swell carried the ships apart, and *Penguin*'s foremast tore loose, falling over her port guns so that they could not be used. Biddle asked if she had struck, whereupon two English seamen fired, wounding him through the neck. U.S. Marines immediately shot them down, and Biddle's officers had difficulty in restraining *Hornet*'s men from slaughtering the entire enemy crew.

The action was over in twenty-two minutes. *Hornet* lost one man killed and eleven wounded, while *Penguin*'s casualties were ten dead and twenty-eight wounded.

Capture of Algerian *Mashouda* and *Estedio* (17 June and 19 June 1815)

During the War of 1812 the United States continued paying tribute to the Mediterranean pirates. When the dey of Algiers sent a ransom note for the captain and crew of the American merchantman *Edwin* in 1815, however, President James Madison decided this matter had to be cleared up once and for all. On 20 May, Capt. Stephen Decatur sailed for the Mediterranean in his flagship *Guerrière,* in command of a squadron composed of *Constellation, Macedonian, Epervier, Ontario, Firefly, Spark, Flambeau, Torch,* and *Spitfire.*

After stopping at Gibraltar, where he learned the Algerians had ships out in force, Decatur entered the Mediterranean. *Mashouda* was spotted first. Cut off from Algeria, she tried to run for a neutral Spanish port. *Constellation* first led the chase, then *Ontario, Guerrière,* and *Epervier* forced *Mashouda*'s surrender. A single American had been killed and 3 wounded by enemy fire, while *Mashouda* lost 30 killed and 406 taken prisoner, including many wounded.

Two days later the pirate brig *Estedio* was sighted and ran immediately into shallow water where the frigates could not follow. *Epervier, Spark, Torch,* and *Spitfire* forced her aground, however, whereupon some of the corsairs escaped by boat. A few broadsides brought surrender, with eighty prisoners taken and thirty wounded found on the brig's decks.

Nine days later Decatur was off Algiers, demanding an indemnity from the dey. News of the capture of these two ships, as related by *Mashouda*'s first officer, convinced the Ottoman official that peace with America, at any price, was worthwhile.

Peacock versus *Nautilus* (30 June 1815)

Having received no word of the peace treaty, *Peacock* was cruising in the Indian Ocean against British commerce when she encountered the fourteen-gun brig *Nautilus*. On coming within hail, British lieutenant Charles Boyce, commanding *Nautilus,* asked Peacock if she had heard of the peace treaty being signed. Capt. Lewis Washington, in *Peacock,* suspected an enemy trick to escape and demanded that the brig surrender, firing one gun when surrender was not forthcoming. *Nautilus* answered with a broadside, and the battle was on. *Peacock* returned the fire, killing six and wounding eight British crewmen, and *Nautilus* struck her colors. No one was wounded or killed in the American ship.

After the surrender, when the rumor of peace was confirmed as fact, Washington carefully repaired the damage to *Nautilus* and returned her to the British.

Core Values

Throughout its history the U.S. Navy has successfully met all its challenges. America's naval service began during the American Revolution, when, on 13 October 1775, the Continental Congress authorized a few small ships, creating the Continental Navy. Esek Hopkins was appointed commander in chief and twenty-two officers, including John Paul Jones, were commissioned.

From those early days of naval service, certain bedrock principles, or core values, have carried on to today. Those three basic principles are honor, courage, and commitment.

Honor

"I will bear true faith and allegiance . . ." Accordingly, we will conduct ourselves in the highest ethical manner in all relationships with peers, superiors, and subordinates; be honest and truthful in our dealings with each other and with those outside the Navy; be willing to make honest recommendations and accept those of junior personnel; encourage new ideas and deliver the bad news, even when it is unpopular; abide by an uncompromising code of integrity, taking responsibility for our actions and keeping our word; fulfill or exceed our legal and ethical responsibilities in our public and personal lives twenty-four hours a day. Illegal or improper behavior or even the appearance of such behavior will not be tolerated. We are accountable for our professional and personal behavior. We will be mindful of the privilege to serve our fellow Americans.

Courage

"I will support and defend . . ." Accordingly, we will have courage to meet the demands of our profession and the mission when it is hazardous, demanding, or otherwise difficult; make decisions in the best interest of the Navy and the nation, without regard to personal consequences; meet these challenges while adhering to a higher standard of personal conduct and decency; be loyal to our nation, ensuring the resources entrusted to us are used in an honest, careful, and efficient way. Courage is the value that gives us the moral and mental strength to do what is right, even in the face of personal or professional adversity.

Commitment

"I will obey the orders . . ." Accordingly, we will demand respect up and down the chain of command; care for the safety and professional, personal, and spiritual well-being of our people; show respect toward all people without regard to race, religion, or gender; treat each individual with human dignity; be committed to positive change and constant improvement; exhibit the highest degree of moral character, technical excellence, quality, and competence in what we have been trained to do. The day-to-day duty of every Navy man and woman is to work together as a team to improve the quality of our work, our people, and ourselves.

Sailor's Creed 22

I am a United States Sailor.

I will support and defend the Constitution of the United States of America and I will obey the orders of those appointed over me.

I represent the fighting spirit of the Navy and those who have gone before me to defend freedom and democracy around the world.

I proudly serve my country's Navy combat team with honor, courage, and commitment.

I am committed to excellence and the fair treatment of all.

Oaths of Office

23

The following sections provide the oaths of office for officer and enlisted personnel of the armed forces of the United States. A detailed history and explanation of the oaths can be found at http://www.airpower.maxwell.af.mil/airchronicles/apj/apj02/win02/keskel.html

Officer Oath

I, _____, do solemnly swear (or affirm) that I will support and defend the Constitution of the United States against all enemies, foreign and domestic; that I will bear true faith and allegiance to the same; that I take this obligation freely, without any mental reservation or purpose of evasion; and that I will well and faithfully discharge the duties of the office on which I am about to enter. So help me God.

Enlisted Oath

I, _____, do solemnly swear (or affirm) that I will support and defend the Constitution of the United States against all enemies, foreign and domestic; that I will bear true faith and allegiance to the same; and that I will obey the orders of the president of the United States and the orders of the officers appointed over me, according to regulations and the Uniform Code of Military Justice. So help me God.

Anthems and Hymns

24

National Anthem: "The Star-Spangled Banner"

An audio file can be found at:
  http://www.bupers.navy.mil/navymusic/audio.htm
  and
  http://bands.army.mil/history/music/nationalanthem.asp

Verse 1

Oh say can you see by the dawn's early light,
What so proudly we hailed at the twilight's last gleaming?
Whose broad stripes and bright stars through the perilous
    fight,
O'er the ramparts we watched were so gallantly streaming?
And the rockets' red glare, the bombs bursting in air,
Gave proof through the night that our flag was still there.
Oh say, does that star-spangled banner yet wave
O'er the land of the free and the home of the brave?

Verse 2

On the shore, dimly seen through the mists of the deep,
Where the foe's haughty host in dread silence reposes,
What is that which the breeze, o'er the towering steep,
As it fitfully blows, half conceals, half discloses?
Now it catches the gleam of the morning's first beam,
In full glory reflected now shines on the stream:
'Tis the star-spangled banner! Oh long may it wave
O'er the land of the free and the home of the brave.

Verse 3

And where is that band who so vauntingly swore
That the havoc of war and the battle's confusion,
A home and a country should leave us no more?
Their blood has washed out their foul footsteps' pollution.
No refuge could save the hireling and slave

From the terror of flight or the gloom of the grave:
And the star-spangled banner in triumph doth wave
O'er the land of the free and the home of the brave.

Verse 4

Oh! thus be it ever, when freemen shall stand
Between their loved homes and the war's desolation!
Blest with victory and peace, may the heav'n rescued land
Praise the Power that hath made and preserved us a nation.
Then conquer we must, when our cause it is just,
And this be our motto: "In God is our trust."
And the star-spangled banner in triumph shall wave
O'er the land of the free and the home of the brave.

"Anchors Aweigh"

A history of "Anchors Aweigh," as well as audio files from the U.S. Navy Band, can be found at: http://www.chinfo.navy.mil/na vpalib/traditions/music/anchor1.html

Original Lyrics

Verse 1

Stand Navy down the field, sails set to the sky.
We'll never change our course, so Army you steer shy-y-y-y.
Roll up the score, Navy, Anchors Aweigh.
Sail Navy down the field and sink the Army, sink the Army
    Grey.

Verse 2

Get underway, Navy, Decks cleared for the fray,
We'll hoist true Navy Blue So Army down your Grey-y-y-y.
Full speed ahead, Navy; Army heave to,
Furl Black and Grey and Gold and hoist the Navy, hoist the
    Navy Blue.

Verse 3

Blue of the Seven Seas; Gold of God's great sun
Let these our colors be Till all of time be done-n-n-ne,
By Severn shore we learn Navy's stern call:
Faith, courage, service true With honor over, honor over all.

Revised Lyrics

Verse 1

Stand, Navy, out to sea, Fight our battle cry;
We'll never change our course, So vicious foe steer shy-y-y-y.
Roll out the TNT, Anchors Aweigh. Sail on to victory
And sink their bones to Davy Jones, hooray!

Verse 2

Anchors Aweigh, my boys, Anchors Aweigh.
Farewell to college joys, we sail at break of day-ay-ay-ay.
Through our last night on shore, drink to the foam,
Until we meet once more. Here's wishing you a happy voy-
age home.

Marine Corps Hymn

An audio file can be found at: http://www.marineband.usmc.mil/
audio_resources/index.htm

Verse 1

From the Halls of Montezuma
To the Shores of Tripoli;
We fight our country's battles
In the air, on land, and sea.
First to fight for right and freedom
And to keep our honor clean;
We are proud to claim the title
of United States Marines.

Verse 2

Our flag's unfurled to every breeze
From dawn to setting sun;
We have fought in every clime and place
Where we could take a gun;
In the snow of far off northern lands
And in sunny tropic scenes;
You will find us always on the job—
The United States Marines.

Verse 3

Here's health to you and to our Corps
Which we are proud to serve
In many a strife we've fought for life
And never lost our nerve;
If the Army and the Navy
Ever look on Heaven's scenes;
They will find the streets are guarded
By United States Marines.

Navy Hymn—"Eternal Father, Strong to Save"

An audio file can be found at:
http://www.chinfo.navy.mil/navpalib/questions/eternal.html

Verse 1

Eternal Father, strong to save,
Whose arm hath bound the restless wave,
Who bidd'st the mighty Ocean deep
Its own appointed limits keep;
Oh, hear us when we cry to Thee,
For those in peril on the sea!

Verse 2

O Christ! Whose voice the waters heard
And hushed their raging at Thy word,
Who walked'st on the foaming deep,
And calm amidst its rage didst sleep;
Oh, hear us when we cry to Thee,
For those in peril on the sea!

Verse 3

Most Holy Spirit! Who didst brood
Upon the chaos dark and rude,
And bid its angry tumult cease,
And give, for wild confusion, peace;
Oh, hear us when we cry to Thee,
For those in peril on the sea!

Verse 4

O Trinity of love and power!
Our brethren shield in danger's hour;
From rock and tempest, fire and foe,
Protect them wheresoe'er they go;
Thus evermore shall rise to Thee,
Glad hymns of praise from land and sea.

Appendix: Ranks of the Armed Forces

Officer and Enlisted Ranks Insignia

RANKS OF THE ARMED FORCES

Navy and Coast Guard
Officer Ranks

Captain
O-6

**Admiral / Commandant
of the Coast Guard**
O-10

Commander
O-5

Vice Admiral
O-9

Lieutenant Commander
O-4

Rear Admiral
(Upper Half)
O-8

Lieutenant
O-3

Rear Admiral
(Lower Half)
O-7

Lieutenant Junior Grade
O-2

Ensign
O-1

Navy, Army, Air Force, Marine Corps, and Coast Guard Officer Ranks

Captain/Colonel
O-6

 Silver

**Commander/
Lieutenant Colonel**
O-5

 Gold

**Lieutenant Commander/
Major**
O-4

Lieutenant/Captain
O-3

 Silver

**Lieutenant Junior Grade/
First Lieutenant**
O-2

Gold

Ensign/Second Lieutenant
O-1

**Fleet Admiral (Navy)/
General of the
Air Force/Army**
(Reserved for Wartime)
O-10

Admiral/General
O-10

**Vice Admiral/
Lieutenant General**
O-9

**Rear Admiral (upper half)/
Major General**
O-8

**Rear Admiral (lower half)/
Brigadier General**
O-7

Navy, Coast Guard, and Marine Corps Warrant Officer Ranks

Navy & Coast Guard	Marine Corps

Chief Warrant Officer 5
W-5

Chief Warrant Officer 5
W-5

Chief Warrant Officer 4
W-4

Chief Warrant Officer 4
W-4

Chief Warrant Officer 3
W-3

Chief Warrant Officer 3
W-3

Chief Warrant Officer 2
W-2

Chief Warrant Officer 2
W-2

Warrant Officer 1
(Coast Guard only)
W-1

Warrant Officer 1
W-1

Air Force and Army
Warrant Officer Ranks

Air Force	**Army**

No Warrant	**Chief Warrant Officer 6**
(W-5)	W-5

No Warrant	**Chief Warrant Officer 4**
(W-4)	W-4

No Warrant	**Chief Warrant Officer 3**
(W-3)	W-3

No Warrant	**Chief Warrant Officer 2**
(W-2)	W-2

No Warrant	**Warrant Officer 1**
(W-1)	W-1

Navy and Coast Guard Enlisted Ranks

Petty Officer First Class
E-6

Petty Officer Second Class
E-5

Petty Officer Third Class
E-4

Seaman
E-3

Seaman Apprentice
E-2

Seaman Recruit
E-1

**Master Chief Petty Officer
of the Navy / Coast Guard**
E-9

**Master Chief Petty Officer,
Fleet/Force/Command
Master Chief Petty Officer**
E-9

Senior Chief Petty Officer
E-8

Chief Petty Officer
E-7

Marine Corps Enlisted Ranks

Staff Sergeant
E-6

Sergeant
E-5

Corporal
E-4

Lance Corporal
E-3

Private First Class
E-2

Private
E-1

**Sergeant Major
of the Marine Corps**
E-9

**Sergeant Major,
Master Gunnery Sergeant**
E-9

**First Sergeant,
Master Sergeant**
E-8

Gunnery Sergeant
E-7

Army Enlisted Ranks

Staff Sergeant
E-6

**Sergeant Major
of the Army**
E-9

Sergeant
E-5

**Sergeant Major,
Command
Sergeant Major**
E-9

Corporal, Specialist
E-4

**Master Sergeant,
First Sergeant**
E-8

Private First Class
E-3

Sergeant First Class
E-7

Private
E-2

Private
E-1

Air Force Enlisted Ranks

Technical Sergeant
E-6

Staff Sergeant
E-5

Senior Airman
E-4

Airman First Class
E-3

Airman
E-2

Airman Basic
E-1

**Chief Master Sergeant
of the Air Force**
E-9

**Chief Master Sergeant,
First Sergeant,
Command Chief Master
Sergeant**
E-9

**Senior Master Sergeant,
First Sergeant**
E-8

**Master Sergeant,
First Sergeant**
E-7

Line and Staff Corps Insignia

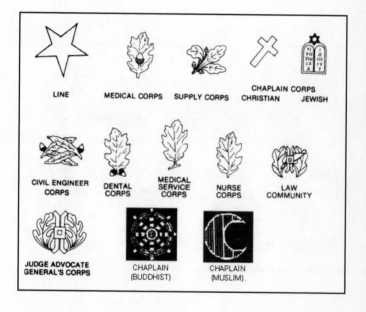

Line and staff corps insignia are worn on both sleeves, above the stripes, and on the shoulder boards. Officers other than line officers also wear them on the collar tips of khaki and blue shirts.

Warrant Officer Insignia

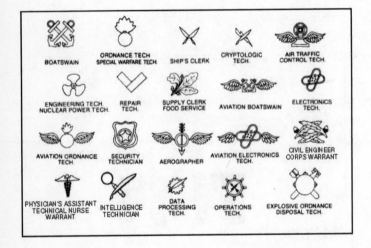

Some of the warrant officer insignia worn on sleeves, above the stripes on sleeves, on shoulder boards, and as pin-on collar devices.

Pins

Some of the warfare and other qualification insignia worn by officers and enlisted personnel.

Index

Note: Page references in *italics* indicate information contained in photographs, captions, and illustrations. The letter *t* following a page number denotes a table. Aircraft are alphabetized by designation.

About the Author

Anthony Cowden attended the University of Michigan under the Navy Reserve Officer Training Corps (NROTC) program, receiving his B.A. degree in History in 1984 and his M.S. degree in Computer Science from the University of New Haven in 2001. After nearly five years on active duty, Mr. Cowden joined Sonalysts, Inc., where he is now a Principal Analyst. Mr. Cowden is a Commander in the Naval Reserve, and on active duty and in the Reserves he has served on five different classes of warship. After 9/11 he was mobilized to OPNAV N3/N5 (Operations and Plans), where he served as Navy Liaison Officer to the Joint Staff and Battle Watch Captain in the Navy Operations Center. He is married to the former Suzanne Johnson and has two sons, Thomas and Robert. He can be reached at navalalmanac@snet.net.

The Naval Institute Press is the book-publishing arm of the U.S. Naval Institute, a private, nonprofit membership society for sea service professionals and others who share an interest in naval and maritime affairs. Established in 1873 at the U.S. Naval Academy in Annapolis, Maryland, where its offices remain today, the Naval Institute has members worldwide.

Members of the Naval Institute support the education programs of the society and receive the influential monthly magazine *Proceedings* and discounts on fine nautical prints and on ship and aircraft photos. They also have access to the transcripts of the Institute's Oral History Program and get discounted admission to any of the Institute-sponsored seminars offered around the country. Discounts are also available to the colorful bimonthly magazine *Naval History*.

The Naval Institute's book-publishing program, begun in 1898 with basic guides to naval practices, has broadened its scope to include books of more general interest. Now the Naval Institute Press publishes about one hundred titles each year, ranging from how-to books on boating and navigation to battle histories, biographies, ship and aircraft guides, and novels. Institute members receive significant discounts on the Press's more than eight hundred books in print.

Full-time students are eligible for special half-price membership rates. Life memberships are also available.

For a free catalog describing Naval Institute Press books currently available, and for further information about joining the U.S. Naval Institute, please write to:

Customer Service
U.S. Naval Institute
291 Wood Road
Annapolis, MD 21402-5034
Telephone: (800) 233-8764
Fax: (410) 269-7940
Web address: www.navalinstitute.org